cook like a pro

# cook like a pro

recipes & tips for home cooks

a barefoot contessa cookbook

# ina garten

Photographs by Quentin Bacon

clarkson potter / publishers

new york

For Barbara Libath, who has been my
"partner in crime" for the past twenty years.
You'll never know how grateful I am.

Library of Congress
Cataloging-in-Publication Data
Names: Garten, Ina, author.
Title: Cook like a pro / Ina Garten.
Description: First edition. |
New York: Clarkson Potter/
Publishers, 2018 | Series: A
Barefoot Contessa cookbook |
Includes index.
Identifiers: LCCN 2018006753|
ISBN 9780804187046 (hard-
cover) | ISBN 9780804187053
(ebook)
Subjects: LCSH: Cooking. |
Barefoot Contessa (Store) |
LCGFT: Cookbooks.

Classification: LCC TX714 .
G36434 2018 | DDC 641.5—dc23
LC record available at https://
lccn.loc.gov/2018006753.

ISBN 978-0-8041-8704-6
Ebook ISBN 978-0-8041-8705-3

Printed in China
Book design by Marysarah Quinn
Photographs by Quentin Bacon

10 9 8 7 6 5 4 3 2 1

First Edition

# contents

# thank you!

It's amazing to think that after writing ten cookbooks, the eleventh can still be so interesting and fun! It's not just that I love what I do every day but also that I love the people who do it with me. First and foremost is my wonderful team: Barbara Libath and Lidey Heuck work on the cookbooks and television shows with me. They're such happy, smart, and thoughtful women and I look forward to seeing them every single day.

Next is my incredible publisher, Clarkson Potter. We've been together since my first book contract in 1997—yikes! My deep thanks go to some of the loveliest and smartest people in the business, which is why when most authors are moving from publisher to publisher, I've stayed put for twenty years. Thank you to Maya Mavjee, the incomparable head of Crown Publishing; to David Drake, who has the best advice about all kinds of things; to Aaron Wehner, the head of Clarkson Potter, who is so wise about cookbooks; to my wonderful editors, Pam Krauss and Raquel Pelzel; my amazing publicist, Kate Tyler; and Marysarah Quinn, the head of design at Crown who so generously still designs all my books herself. Writing cookbooks is definitely a team sport and I'm playing with the A team.

And this is yet another book photographed by the brilliant Quentin Bacon. This time, we had Cyd McDowell (with backup by Christine Albano) preparing beautiful food and Miguel Flores-Vianna, who so graciously agreed to take a break from his gorgeous photography, come back and style for us. We developed a slightly different "in the kitchen" style for this book and I hope you'll like it as much as I do.

Thank you also to my amazing friend and agent, Esther Newberg, who takes care of business so I can do the fun stuff: write cookbooks. And finally to my friend Sarah Leah Chase, who writes her own cookbooks and who inspires me with new ideas and recipes all year long.

# cook with confidence!

When I started my television series on Food Network called *Cook Like a Pro* and decided to write this book, I think a few people might have thought I'd drifted away from what I love most—writing recipes for simple, delicious home cooking. Maybe they imagined I'd be showing you how to make a demi-glace base for a fancy sauce or how to carve a radish rose. Nope, that's never been what my cooking is about! What I think you *will* find, however, is that by following these recipes and "pro tips," your food may taste a little more vibrant, your presentation may be a little more polished, and you may feel a little more confident in your cooking skills; in other words, you'll be cooking the way pros cook! It's a funny paradox that when something from a bakery is delicious, we compliment it by saying, "This tastes homemade!" but when something we make at home is especially impressive, everyone says, "This looks so professional!" With that in mind, my goal with this book is to ensure that everything you cook looks and tastes like it was "homemade by professionals!"

Why is it worth learning to cook the way pros do? Because when you have the right knife and it's perfectly sharpened, you'll find prep work so much easier and more satisfying. When you measure your ingredients precisely (the difference between liquid and dry measures is more important than you think!) or know how to judge when your cake is done or your beef tenderloin is the right temperature for medium rare, you'll find cooking and entertaining so much less stressful. Throughout this book you'll find extra tips that will help you prepare these recipes exactly the way I do, and with fewer unhappy surprises.

In the early days, I taught myself how to cook from cookbooks; Craig Claiborne's *New York Times Cookbook* was my undergraduate education and Julia Child, Louisette Bertholle, and Simone Beck's *Mastering the Art of French Cooking* was graduate school. By making those recipes over and over again and persevering until I got them the way Craig and Julia intended, I learned a million things, from the easiest way to chop an onion to the right way to truss a chicken and how to make a perfect Hollandaise sauce. To this day, the scientist in me loves knowing how something works and that background in the classics was invaluable. But the practical side of me loves newer, fresher, simpler ways to do things—ways that ensure a recipe will come out right the *first* time you make it. Drawing on my experience as a caterer, a specialty food store owner, and of course a cookbook author, I've devised a battery of time-tested tricks that I rely on in the kitchen to make flavors sing and presentation pop. I try to incorporate those tips into every recipe I develop, and I make these recipes dozens of times so that your results will always be just as good as mine.

Since those early days of teaching myself to cook, I've spent years in professional kitchens and have learned so much from the chefs and bakers I worked with. When I ran Barefoot Contessa, needing to peel forty pounds of butternut squash one afternoon taught me the importance of sharp knives and the most efficient way to peel a squash for Butternut Squash Gratin (page 166). When the baker didn't show up for work one night and I had to make fifty Chocolate Chevron Cakes (page 180), I learned the fastest and best way to bake a cake that looks impressive without a lot of extra effort. When I started catering private events, I saw firsthand what makes the best parties. I learned that a happy, relaxed host is the most important ingredient at any gathering—and that small round tables with food served family-style or from a buffet are always the most fun.

Writing cookbooks has added yet another dimension to my experience. I learn so much just developing the recipes but after I'm done testing them, I ask everyone on my team to retest them so I can see how other people cook them. When I've written "sliced carrots," someone will ask me if I meant straight across or diagonally and the answer goes into the recipe. I tease my guys that their job is actually to *make* mistakes so I see what someone at home might do unknowingly. When one of my assistants confused whole garlic cloves with cloves in a lentil soup recipe, I decided to always write "dried cloves" whenever I was referring to the spice, so no one would ever accidentally make that mistake again. If you have a question about a process or an ingredient, you'll probably find the answer is right there in the margin, along with a photo of what it should look like.

# taste like a pro

Following the recipe exactly is the first step in producing really delicious results. But that's not the end of it. When I was a kid, I wanted to cook because I was always searching for flavor. In those days, bread meant Wonder bread and tomatoes came three in a row, side by side in a cello package. They looked identical all year long, and they tasted like the package they came in. My mother didn't particularly love to cook, so while she always put a nice dinner on the table for us, nutrition, not flavor, was her objective. For me, it's *all* about the flavor. Every time I write a new recipe, I ask myself, "Is this *really* delicious?" Is this worth going to the grocery store, buying the ingredients, cooking the dish, and cleaning up afterward? That's a pretty high bar! If you're hungry, you can pick up a pizza or frozen lasagna for dinner almost anywhere, so if you're going to the trouble of actually *cooking* something, it really has to be worth the effort. Hopefully, when you make the recipes in this book, the answer to that question will always be a heartfelt *"YES!"*

In my recipes, every ingredient has to pull its own weight, and I want the flavors to be perfectly layered so no one flavor smacks you in the head while the next one is so subtle that you hardly notice it. Of course, some ingredients need a partner to bring out their flavor, which is why I always put a touch of coffee in my chocolate dishes. You don't taste the coffee but it makes the chocolate taste better. Other ingredients create a pleasing "edge" that brings out all the flavors in a dish. When I'm writing a recipe, I'm often looking for something acidic to wake up the flavors—a splash of red wine vinegar in the Chicken Marbella (page 84), a squeeze of lemon juice in the Pork Souvlaki (page 115), or some orange zest in the Orange-Roasted Rainbow Carrots (page 156). You'd be surprised how that one ingredient transforms a dish from perfectly fine to *WOW!* It also makes a difference *when* in the process you add that acidic ingredient. Often it's cooked into the dish, but in my Pork Posole (page 55) a squeeze of lime juice right at the end is the first flavor that hits your nose and tongue: it wakes you up with the first bite! Try it some time. Make the Israeli Vegetable Salad (page 52) and taste it before and after adding the mint, extra salt, and drizzle of olive oil at the end. You'll be surprised what that final flourish adds to the dish.

That's why it's important always to be engaged when you're cooking. Chefs are constantly tasting things and making adjustments along the way

and you should do the same. There's no way for me to know if the butternut squash you bought is early season, late season, from the grocery store, or from your garden. I can write a recipe for an amazing Fresh Peach Cremolata (page 206), but I can't know if the peaches you're using were picked unripe six weeks ago and shipped from South America or if you just walked outside your front door and picked them off your tree. A friend once called and said the Peach & Raspberry Crisp she made from *The Barefoot Contessa Cookbook* was delicious but it was a little soupy. When I asked what peaches she used, she said that she had made it from juicy, perfectly tree-ripened peaches in her garden. (A little more flour was the solution—I'll bet that was a delicious crisp!) Of course, her crisp was going to cook differently from a peach crisp made from hard grocery store peaches. The more you cook, the better idea you'll have of how things *should* taste and how the ingredients will perform, and those instincts will grow with every recipe you make.

To make it easy to do this kind of tinkering, I keep bowls of ingredients like limes and lemons on my counter next to a crock of sea salt; not only are they better used at room temperature, but while I'm testing a recipe, I don't have to go scrambling for inspiration when I want to add that extra burst of flavor; it's right there in front of me. When you come home from the store, if you have ingredients that don't spoil, don't hide them in your fridge. Put them in matching white bowls on the counter. They'll encourage you to make your own flavor adjustments and, happily, they're also great counter decoration: like a vase of flowers, they make a kitchen feel alive.

# season like a pro

A chef once said to me that the two things many people get wrong in cooking are two things everyone has in their kitchen: salt and pepper. Salt is a really important component of my recipes and part of what makes my cooking taste great. Because it's been associated with high blood pressure for decades (though the new research shows that it may not be as bad as we were told!), salt has gotten a bad rap, but it's what ramps up the flavor of everything you cook—both savory *and* sweet. My Red Berry Shortcakes (page 213) have salt in the biscuits and if you forget to add it, trust me, you'll notice. Anyone who's tried homemade chicken stock made without salt knows it can taste like dirty dishwater. Add a few tablespoons of salt to a huge pot and the deep, rich flavors of chicken, vegetables, and fresh herbs emerge instantly. By the way, homemade Chicken Stock (page 259) is one of the cornerstones of my cooking; it makes all the difference over store-bought stock in the Tomato & Eggplant Soup (page 62).

Of course, you *can* oversalt food but it's more likely that you've been undersalting it. If I'm not sure about how much salt a dish needs, instead of salting the entire pot and risk oversalting it, I'll put a little of what I'm cooking into a small bowl, add some salt, and see how it changes the flavor. That way I can add salt slowly and carefully without ruining the whole dish (after all, you can always add more but you can't take it out!). Happily, salt is also probably the cheapest ingredient you have in your kitchen so don't neglect it!

# plate like a pro

Another trick every pro knows is that we eat with our eyes as well as our mouths, and a beautiful presentation sets up an expectation that a dish will taste amazing before you even take a bite. As a former specialty food store owner and caterer, I've been plating up food for decades so it's second nature to me, but you may need to experiment a bit. Plating food is a little like arranging flowers in a vase. You want to make the flowers look better; you don't want to find yourself admiring the vase! The same is true for platters and food. After

trying all kinds of patterned plates and platters (I'm a sucker for Chinese blue and white dishes), I concluded that, with a few exceptions, simple white serving pieces make the colors in the food pop best. You can find plain white bowls and platters at any cookware store, home store, or restaurant supply outlet.

Next, how do you fill the platters? Again, as with flowers, you don't want to see a vase crammed with flowers, nor do you want the flowers to flop around in a vase that's too big. Serving platters are no different. You want platters to showcase the food and make it look better than you imagined. I do this by arranging the food so the platter is full but still has a white border around the food—almost like a picture frame. I don't love to serve from deep bowls; I think they hide the food. Instead, I prefer big, wide, shallow bowls that are perfect for salads and vegetables; for meats and fish, I use white oval or round platters. I find a square piece of meat, such as a pork shoulder, looks best on a round platter and a long narrow piece, such as beef tenderloin, looks best on an oval platter.

Using tricks like these, you can easily make something homemade look totally impressive and professional. Instead of serving the Baked Pasta with Tomatoes & Eggplant (page 83) in one ceramic baking dish, I bake it in individual gratin dishes. Not only does it taste better (there are more crusty bits on top!) but it also feels so much more special. The same is true for desserts; instead of serving the Campari & Orange Granita (page 178) in an ordinary dessert bowl, I put it into stemmed martini glasses and voilà!—a beautiful, elegant dessert. It's not any more work, and the presentation just says it all.

Good food is a little like couture fashion. The simpler it is, the better. When designers start with gorgeous fabric, they don't have to add all kinds of trimmings and bows to make a beautiful dress. With cooking, when you start with good ingredients, often all you need is a simple preparation to make them taste wonderful. My guests are always happy to find that I'm serving something comforting like Red Wine–Braised Short Ribs (page 119) and I know that a tried-and-true dish like this one will satisfy them without stressing me out. If people feel that you're relaxed and happy, they will have a wonderful time. And isn't that why you invited them in the first place?

I love the way the desire to cook and share food with the people that are important to us transcends class, gender, age, and ethnicity. *Everyone* is interested in food. I was walking on the street in New York City one day and a very posh woman in a big fur coat waved at me and said, "Darling, love your cookbooks!" A block later, a truck driver pulled over to the curb and yelled out the window, "Hey babe, love your show!" Good food truly is a universal language we all understand. My goal with this book is that everyone will have the tools and information to cook totally delicious and professional-looking dishes every time. And even better—your family and friends will love you for it! How great is that?

xxx's Ina

# cocktails

# arrange a bar like a pro

I was a caterer for decades and, no matter how many guests there were, I always set up the bar the same way. Of course, for large parties there was a bartender to make the drinks, but the same arrangement works as well for a self-service bar, and to this day I use the same system at home when I entertain.

You want everything you need on the table so you don't have to scurry to the kitchen every time a new guest arrives. This isn't the time to empty your liquor cabinet—write a bar menu and stick to it. I like to have one mixed cocktail like whiskey sours premade in a pitcher or a bottle of Champagne in a bucket of ice and water, plus vodka, bourbon, scotch, rum, and gin. Make sure there is plenty of ice and a bowl of fruit for garnishes.

I set a table against a wall with a row of spirits, wine, mixers, and juices at the back, all lined up with the labels facing out. In front of these, I place the glasses; two or three kinds are usually enough. If I'm renting glasses, I'll just order hand-blown stemmed all-purpose wine and Champagne glasses. (Renting glasses isn't terribly expensive and guess what? You don't need to wash them before you send them back!) Allow two glasses per person.

I arrange the glasses in a triangle, with the first row at the back of the table, in front of the spirits and mixers. The second row is one glass shorter at each end and so on until you have a tight triangle of glasses in very straight rows. If you have a large number of glasses, you can arrange them in two triangles, instead of one.

To finish the bar, put a pretty dish of crudités or salted nuts in front and, if there's room, a vase of flowers. The good news is that you can set this all up a day in advance and just fill the pitchers and ice bucket on the day of the party. I love to see people making drinks for themselves and then for each other, catching up, and getting the party started all by themselves!

# autumn sangria

makes 8 to 10 drinks

*Bobby Flay is one of the most natural cooks I've ever known. When Jeffrey and I first moved to New York, we lived across the street from his first restaurant, Mesa Grill, which we loved. Bobby made this sangria for me with spicy red wine, lots of autumn fruit, and cinnamon syrup, and I've been making it ever since. This is my kind of recipe—the sweet fruit makes the spiced wine taste better and the wine makes the fruit taste better.*

½ cup sugar

4 (3-inch) whole cinnamon sticks

1 (750-ml) bottle Cabernet Sauvignon

1½ cups fresh apple cider

¼ cup plus 2 tablespoons apple brandy, such as Calvados

¼ cup plus 2 tablespoons pear brandy

1 small (or ½ large) Gala or Fuji apple, halved, cored, and
    thinly sliced crosswise

1 Granny Smith apple, halved, cored, and thinly sliced crosswise

1 small (or ½ regular) red Bartlett pear, halved, cored, and
    thinly sliced crosswise

1 small (or ½ regular) green Bartlett pear, halved, cored, and
    thinly sliced crosswise

¼ cup pomegranate seeds (see tip)

½ orange, halved through the stem end and thinly sliced
    crosswise

**pro tip** Seed a pomegranate by cutting it in half, holding it over parchment paper or a bowl, cut side down, and whacking the skin with a wooden spoon. The seeds will just pop out.

For the cinnamon syrup, combine the sugar and ½ cup water in a small saucepan. Bring to a boil over high heat and cook for 3 minutes, until the sugar dissolves completely. Cool, transfer to a container, add the cinnamon sticks, cover, and chill for at least 4 hours or for up to 48 hours. The longer it sits, the more intense the flavor will be.

In a large (2-quart) pitcher, combine the wine, apple cider, apple brandy, pear brandy, ½ cup of the cinnamon syrup, and all of the fruit. Cover and refrigerate for at least 4 hours or up to 72 hours. Fill wine goblets ¾ full with ice, pour in the sangria, and spoon some of the macerated fruit into each glass. Serve ice cold.

# bay scallop ceviche

serves 4 to 6

*When making ceviche, the quality of the scallops makes all the difference so be sure to buy fresh (not frozen) scallops. There is no cooking involved; the raw scallops will "cook" in the lime juice in just one hour (less time and the scallops will be too raw; more time and they'll get mushy). When scallops are in season, the combination of the briny scallops, citrusy lime juice, and all those fresh vegetables make this a great appetizer.*

¾ pound bay scallops (or sea scallops, cut in quarters),
  muscles removed
¾ cup freshly squeezed lime juice, divided (5 limes)
Kosher salt and freshly ground black pepper
1 cup (½ to ¾-inch diced) hothouse cucumber, unpeeled
  and seeded
½ cup halved and thinly sliced shallots (2 shallots)
3 tablespoons diagonally sliced scallions, white and green parts
½ Hass avocado, ¾-inch diced
½ cup Holland red bell pepper, ½ to ¾-inch diced
¼ cup roughly chopped fresh parsley
1½ tablespoons minced jalapeño pepper (see tip)
1½ teaspoons minced garlic (2 cloves)
Good olive oil
¼ teaspoon Sriracha
Bibb lettuce leaves, for serving

**pro tip** For flavor without overwhelming heat, just use the flesh of the jalapeño. Cut it in half lengthwise and remove the seeds and ribs before mincing. The oils will get on your hands; be sure to wash them afterward!

In a medium bowl, combine the scallops, ½ cup of the lime juice, and 1 teaspoon salt and set aside at room temperature for exactly 1 hour, stirring occasionally.

In a separate bowl, combine the cucumbers, shallots, scallions, avocado, bell pepper, parsley, jalapeño pepper, and garlic. In a glass measuring cup, whisk together the remaining ¼ cup lime juice, ¼ cup olive oil, 1 teaspoon salt, ½ teaspoon pepper, and the Sriracha. Pour over the vegetables and combine.

When ready to serve, lift the scallops out of the lime juice with a slotted spoon (discard the liquid) and add them to the vegetable mixture. Stir well and spoon into the lettuce leaves for serving.

# classic daiquiris, updated

makes 6 drinks

*In the 1960s everyone drank these sophisticated rum drinks, but then bar-tenders started adding sweet things like strawberries and bananas and blend-ing them with ice, making them more like spiked smoothies than cocktails. I decided to revisit the original, made with lots of freshly squeezed lime juice. My friend, bartender Michael Sturgis, suggested that I use Bacardi Gold rum and it makes all the difference!*

**1 cup sugar, plus extra for dipping the glasses**
**1 lime, cut in half**
**1⅓ cups freshly squeezed lime juice (9 limes)**
**1⅓ cups Bacardi Gold dark rum**
**Very thin whole slices of lime, for serving**

Combine the sugar with 1 cup water in a small saucepan and heat until the sugar dissolves completely. Set aside to cool or refrigerate for up to 2 weeks.

When ready to make the cocktails, rub the cut lime on the rims of 6 glasses and lightly dip the rims in a plate of sugar. Turn the glasses upright and set aside to dry.

Combine the lime juice, 1 cup of the sugar syrup, and the rum in a pitcher. Fill a cocktail shaker ¾ full with ice, pour in enough cocktail mixture to cover the ice, place the lid on the shaker, and shake for a full 30 seconds, until very cold. (Time it; it's longer than you think!) Fill the prepared glasses ¾ full with ice and strain the daiquiris into the glasses, garnish with the lime slices, and serve ice cold. Repeat until you've used all of the cocktail mixture.

**pro tip** Limes at room temperature give more juice than cold ones. Roll the whole limes on a board with the heel of your hand before squeezing them to release more juice.

# warm dates
## with blue cheese & prosciutto

makes 24 appetizers; serves 6

*Lidey Heuck, who works with me, suggested this combination as an appetizer to serve with drinks. They're not the prettiest things in the world but they're so easy to make, and the combination of the sweet dates, sharp blue cheese, and salty prosciutto knocks everyone out.*

**24 large dried Medjool dates with pits (14 ounces)**
**6 ounces sharp blue cheese, such as Bleu d'Auvergne**
**¼ pound thinly sliced prosciutto (8 to 10 large slices)**

Preheat the oven to 400 degrees.

With a small paring knife, slit each date lengthwise and spread open just enough to remove the pit while leaving the date intact. Fill the cavity of each date with a small piece of blue cheese and fold the date over the cheese, pressing it back into its original shape.

Cut a strip of prosciutto as wide as each date is long and wrap it around twice, enclosing the date almost completely. Place the dates on a sheet pan and bake for about 8 minutes, until the prosciutto is browned and the cheese starts to melt.

Cool slightly and serve warm.

**Look for dried Medjool dates in the produce section of your grocery store; they will be the freshest.**

**pro tip** If the cold prosciutto sticks to the paper, heat it in the microwave for a few seconds.

# roasted shrimp cocktail louis

serves 8 to 10

*This dish was invented in 1915 at the St. Francis Hotel in San Francisco. It's shrimp cocktail but instead of tomato horseradish sauce, the hotel's sauce was more like a spicy Russian dressing. This is my jazzed-up version of that dish. Roasting rather than boiling the shrimp makes them so tender and flavorful.*

2 pounds large (16 to 20-count) shrimp, peeled, deveined, with the tails on (see tip, page 131)

Good olive oil

Kosher salt and freshly ground black pepper

1¼ cups good mayonnaise, such as Hellmann's

½ cup Heinz chili sauce

½ teaspoon grated lemon zest

2 tablespoons freshly squeezed lemon juice

1½ tablespoons bottled grated white horseradish, drained

2 teaspoons Sriracha

1 teaspoon Worcestershire sauce

¼ cup minced scallions (2 scallions)

2 tablespoons capers, drained

**make ahead:** The dipping sauce can be made ahead and refrigerated for up to 3 days.

Preheat the oven to 400 degrees.

Dry the shrimp well with paper towels. Place them on a sheet pan with 1 tablespoon olive oil, 1 teaspoon salt, and ½ teaspoon pepper, toss well, and spread them out in one layer. Roast for 10 minutes, until firm and just cooked through. Set aside to cool.

Meanwhile, in a medium bowl, whisk together the mayonnaise, chili sauce, lemon zest, lemon juice, horseradish, Sriracha, Worcestershire sauce, 1 teaspoon salt, and ½ teaspoon pepper. Stir in the scallions and capers. Arrange the shrimp on a platter with the sauce in the middle for dipping. Offer a separate bowl for the discarded shrimp tails.

# sausage & mushroom strudels

serves 8 to 10

*I've been making a version of this dish for decades. It's a substantial appetizer to serve with drinks and also delicious as part of a buffet. The spicy sausage and earthy cremini mushrooms combined with onion, fennel seeds, and a little rich mascarpone are so good together!*

**½ pound sweet Italian sausage links, casings removed**
**½ pound chicken sausage links, casings removed**
**16 tablespoons (2 sticks) unsalted butter, divided**
**1 cup chopped yellow onion**
**1 pound cremini mushrooms**
**1 teaspoon whole fennel seeds**
**Kosher salt and freshly ground black pepper**
**1 (8.8-ounce) package Italian mascarpone cheese, at room**
    **temperature**
**½ cup fresh bread crumbs (see tip)**
**1 package (24 sheets) Kontos phyllo dough, defrosted**
**Plain dry bread crumbs, such as Progresso**

**pro tip** Fresh bread crumbs stay moister in the filling than dry ones. Dry bread crumbs keep the phyllo dough flaky. To make your own fresh bread crumbs, remove the crusts from sliced white bread, cube the bread, and place it in the bowl of a food processor fitted with the steel blade. Process until the bread is in fine crumbs.

Preheat the oven to 400 degrees. Line a sheet pan with parchment paper.

If either of the sausage meats is coarsely ground, place the meat in the bowl of a food processor fitted with the steel blade, and pulse until the meat is finely ground.

Heat 4 tablespoons of the butter in a large (12-inch) sauté pan, add the onion, and cook for 4 to 6 minutes over medium heat, until tender but not browned. Add all the sausage meat and mash with a fork, breaking it up and browning it, for 5 to 7 minutes, until no longer pink.

Meanwhile, prep the mushrooms. Without washing the mushrooms, wipe the caps with a slightly damp paper towel or sponge to remove any dirt. Trim the stems, then roughly chop the caps and stems. Add the mushrooms, fennel seeds, 1 teaspoon salt, and 1 teaspoon pepper to the sausage and cook for 10 minutes, until the mushrooms give off their liquid and the liquid evaporates. Set aside to cool for 10 minutes. Stir in the mascarpone and the fresh bread crumbs and season to taste. The seasoning will depend on how highly seasoned the sausage meat is.

Melt the remaining 12 tablespoons of butter in a small saucepan. Unfold the phyllo dough and keep it covered with a slightly damp (not wet!) kitchen towel. Transfer one sheet of phyllo to a board, brush it lightly with melted butter, and sprinkle with a teaspoon of dry bread crumbs. Place a second sheet of phyllo directly on top, brush with butter, and sprinkle with dry bread crumbs; repeat until you have 5 sheets piled up. With the long edge of the stack of phyllo facing you, make a 1-inch strip of sausage filling (about ⅓ of the filling) near the bottom edge. Fold up the sides and roll the phyllo firmly up and over, rolling the log away from you. Transfer the log, seam side down, to the prepared sheet pan. Brush with butter and score diagonally at 1-inch intervals. Make two more strudel logs and place them on the sheet pan.

Bake the strudels for 20 to 30 minutes, rotating the pan once to cook evenly, until browned. Cool slightly, cut in pieces through the scored lines, and serve warm.

**make ahead:** Refrigerate the unsliced unbaked rolls, covered, for up to 5 days or wrap tightly and freeze for up to 4 months. Bake just before serving.

# sautéed shishito peppers

serves 4 to 6

*I've only recently discovered shishito peppers, which look as though they would be hot, but in fact, almost all of them are sweet. (Of course, I always get the hot one!) This is the easiest healthy appetizer to make and you can pick up a charred pepper by the stem and eat the whole thing, seeds and all.*

**Good olive oil**
**½ pound shishito peppers**
**Kosher salt and freshly ground black pepper**
**½ lime**
**Flaked sea salt, such as Maldon**

Heat 2 tablespoons olive oil in a large (12-inch) sauté pan over medium to medium-high heat. When the oil is hot, add the whole peppers in one layer and sprinkle them with 1 teaspoon kosher salt and ½ teaspoon black pepper. Cook for 4 to 6 minutes, tossing often until blistered and browned. Off the heat, squeeze some lime juice on the peppers and sprinkle with flaked sea salt. Serve hot right from the pan or transfer to a small serving dish. Have a dish nearby for discarding the stems.

**pro tip** Acids such as lime juice, lemon juice, and vinegar often add a delicious edge to savory foods like these peppers and give them more depth of flavor.

# smoky eggplant dip
## with yogurt & mint

serves 6

*I'm a total fan of Yotam Ottolenghi, the Israeli-British owner of Ottolenghi London specialty food stores and the restaurant NOPI, and author of many amazing cookbooks. He inspired me to grill eggplants, and then puree them with yogurt, lemon, mint, and garlic. It's a variation of the classic Middle Eastern appetizer baba ganoush.*

2½ pounds eggplant (2 medium)
¼ cup plain whole milk Greek yogurt
2 tablespoons freshly squeezed lemon juice
2 tablespoons julienned fresh mint leaves, plus extra for serving
1 tablespoon minced garlic (3 cloves)
Good olive oil
½ teaspoon Sriracha
Kosher salt and freshly ground black pepper
Grilled or toasted pita triangles, for serving

Make a fire on one side of a charcoal grill. When the fire is hot, prick the eggplants all over with a fork, and place them on the hot side of the grill for 10 minutes, turning occasionally, to char the skin all over. Move the eggplants to the cool side of the grill, put on the lid, making sure the vents are open, and roast the eggplants for 40 to 45 minutes, until they collapse when you press on them, turning once halfway through. Transfer the eggplants to a platter and cut in half lengthwise, allowing any liquid to run out.

With a slotted spoon, scoop the insides of the eggplants into the bowl of a food processor fitted with the steel blade, discarding the skin and any excess liquid. Add the yogurt, lemon juice, mint, garlic, 1 tablespoon olive oil, the Sriracha, 2 teaspoons salt, and 1 teaspoon pepper. Pulse *just* five or six times to combine but not puree the ingredients. Taste for seasonings; it should be highly seasoned!

Transfer to a shallow serving bowl, drizzle with olive oil, sprinkle with extra mint and salt, and serve warm or at room temperature with pita triangles.

**pro tip** If you prefer to roast the eggplant in the oven, prick them all over with the tines of a fork, place on a sheet pan lined with aluminum foil, and roast at 425 degrees for 45 minutes, until they collapse when you press the top. The dip won't be smoky but it will still be delicious.

# warm marinated olives

serves 10

*Many years ago, Jeffrey took me to Milan, a city I simply adore! There is a specialty food store there called Peck, which had a rosticceria (rotisserie store) with all sorts of meats twirling over the largest wood-burning fire you've ever seen. On the counter was a display of every roasted Italian vegetable imaginable, including warm roasted olives, which I'd never seen before. I like to serve them with cocktails before dinner. They're so much more flavorful than olives straight from the fridge!*

2 cups large green olives with pits, such as Cerignola (11 ounces)

2 cups large black olives with pits, such as Kalamata (11 ounces)

Zest of 1 orange, peeled in large strips

4 large garlic cloves, smashed

2 teaspoons whole fennel seeds

2 teaspoons chopped fresh thyme leaves

¾ teaspoon crushed red pepper flakes

Kosher salt and freshly ground black pepper

⅔ cup good olive oil

4 sprigs fresh thyme

Drain the green and black olives from the brine or oil that they're packed in and place them in a medium bowl. Add the orange zest, garlic, fennel seeds, thyme leaves, red pepper flakes, ½ teaspoon salt, and ½ teaspoon black pepper. Pour the olive oil over the mixture, add the thyme sprigs, and toss to combine.

Transfer the mixture, including the olive oil, to a medium (10-inch) sauté pan. Heat over medium heat until the oil begins to sizzle. Lower the heat and sauté for 4 to 5 minutes, stirring occasionally, until the olives and garlic are heated through and fragrant. Serve warm right from the pan or transfer to a serving dish. Offer a small dish for the pits.

**pro tip** This dish depends on the flavor and texture of the olives. Use high-quality olives with pits rather than the canned, pitted ones.

**make ahead:** Combine all the ingredients, cover with plastic wrap, and refrigerate for up to a week. Sauté before serving.

soups &
salads

# measure like a pro

I often wonder if half the reason some people think they can't cook is that they don't measure their ingredients properly. There are so many ways to measure ingredients and a few extra tablespoons of flour or too little liquid can make all the difference between a good outcome and one that is disappointing. If you measure accurately, your recipes will come out the same way every time—no surprises!

The first thing to know is the difference between wet and dry measures. Liquid ingredients such as milk, water, cream, lemon juice, and honey settle level, so they can be poured into a glass measuring cup. For accuracy you want the liquid smack on the line.

For dry ingredients—flour, sugar, rice, salt—you want to fill the cup or measuring spoon, then level off the top with the back of a knife. Some "wet" ingredients such as sour cream or yogurt don't settle level in a measuring cup intended for liquids, so it's best to spoon them into dry cup measures and level them, tapping them on the counter to release any air pockets.

Unless the recipe specifies "packed," as for brown sugar, you generally want dry ingredients like flour or confectioners' sugar to be light and fluffy. If you fill a cup of flour and tap it on the counter, it compresses, so you will need to add more flour to fill the cup. The result is too much flour. Working in a professional kitchen taught me that if you fluff the flour before dipping in your measuring cup and leveling off the top, you will have exactly the same amount of flour each time. Trust me, it makes all the difference when you're baking a cake or thickening a sauce.

Lastly, read how the ingredients are worded. There is a difference between "1 cup chopped pecans" (the nuts are measured *after* they're chopped) and "1 cup pecans, chopped" (you measure the whole pecans and *then* chop them). In my recipes you'll often see two separate measures. "1½ cups chopped onions (1 large)" tells you first how much onion to put in the recipe (1½ cups) and secondly, what to buy at the store (1 large onion). Be sure to use *only* the first amount in the recipe.

Try making these adjustments and I think you'll find that your cooking gets better immediately. And doesn't that give us all the confidence to cook again another day?

**TEASPOONS + TABLESPOONS**

Be sure to use level measures.

**DRY MEASURE**

Use a straight edge, like the back of a knife, to level off the contents of your measuring cups and spoons.

**LIQUID MEASURE**

Lean down to read the measure at eye level.

**SCALE**

Use a scale to accurately measure weights.

# charlie bird's farro salad

serves 6

*My friend Peter Wallace made this for Jeffrey and me for lunch one day and we adored it! The dish originated at the New York City restaurant Charlie Bird, then Melissa Clark loved it so much she published the recipe in her* New York Times *column, and while I've made a few tweaks of my own, it's basically Charlie Bird's creation. I could happily eat this for lunch every day.*

1 cup pearled farro (6 ounces)
1 cup fresh apple cider
2 bay leaves
Kosher salt and freshly ground black pepper
½ cup good olive oil
¼ cup freshly squeezed lemon juice
½ cup roasted, salted pistachios, whole or chopped
1 cup roughly chopped fresh parsley
1 cup roughly chopped fresh mint leaves
1 cup cherry or grape tomatoes, halved through the stem
⅓ cup thinly sliced radishes (2 to 3 radishes)
2 cups baby arugula
½ cup shaved Italian Parmesan cheese (see tip)
Flaked sea salt, such as Maldon

**pro tip** Shave the Parmesan with a vegetable peeler to get large beautiful curls.

Place the farro, apple cider, bay leaves, 2 teaspoons salt, and 2 cups water in a medium saucepan, bring to a boil, lower the heat, and simmer uncovered for about 30 minutes, until the farro is tender. (If all the liquid is absorbed before the farro is tender, add a little more water.) Drain the farro and transfer to a large serving bowl. Discard the bay leaves.

Meanwhile, in a small measuring cup, whisk together the olive oil, lemon juice, 1 teaspoon salt, and ½ teaspoon pepper. Stir the vinaigrette into the warm farro and set aside for at least 15 minutes to cool.

Before serving, stir in the pistachios, parsley, mint, tomatoes, and radishes. Add the arugula and lightly fold in the Parmesan so as not to break it up too much. Sprinkle with the sea salt and serve immediately.

# chicken & spinach waldorf salad

serves 4 to 6

*There's a restaurant in East Hampton, New York, called the East Hampton Grill and whenever I go I order their amazing chicken and spinach Waldorf salad. I was thrilled when* Bon Appétit *magazine published their recipe! We tested and retested this so many times—not because it wasn't perfect, but because we wanted to eat it for lunch!*

1½ pounds bone-in, skin-on chicken breasts (2 large)

⅔ cup good olive oil, plus extra for roasting the chicken

Kosher salt and freshly ground black pepper

½ pound thick-cut bacon, such as Nodine's

¼ cup whole roasted, salted Marcona almonds

¼ cup whole roasted, salted cashews

¼ cup whole walnut halves

3 tablespoons apple cider vinegar

1 tablespoon good Dijon mustard

2 teaspoons liquid honey

4 cups baby frisée, washed, spun dry, and sliced in 1½-inch pieces

4 cups curly kale, ribs removed, washed, spun dry, stacked, and thinly sliced crosswise

4 ounces baby spinach, washed and spun dry

½ cup golden raisins

6 ounces extra-sharp Cheddar, grated

1 crisp red apple, unpeeled

4 soft-boiled eggs, peeled and quartered (see tip)

**pro tip** For soft-boiled eggs, place the eggs in a medium saucepan of boiling water, lower the heat, and simmer for exactly 6 minutes. Set aside for 2 minutes.

Preheat the oven to 350 degrees. Arrange three racks evenly spaced in the oven. If you only have two racks, space them evenly.

Place the chicken, skin side up, on a sheet pan. Rub with olive oil, sprinkle with salt and pepper, and roast for 35 to 40 minutes, until the internal temperature is 140 degrees. Cover the pan with foil and set aside to cool for 10 minutes. Discard the skin and bones, and shred the chicken by hand into 1 × 3-inch pieces.

Place the bacon on a wire cooling rack set on a second sheet pan and roast along with the chicken for 20 to 30 minutes, until browned. Remove the bacon to a plate lined with paper towels, cool, and cut in large dice.

On a third sheet pan, combine the almonds, cashews, and walnuts and roast for 10 to 12 minutes, tossing once, until lightly browned. Set aside to cool.

In a 2-cup measuring cup, whisk the ⅔ cup of olive oil with the vinegar, mustard, honey, 1½ teaspoons salt, and ½ teaspoon pepper, and set aside.

In a large serving bowl, combine the frisée, kale, spinach, raisins, Cheddar, chicken, bacon, nuts, 1 teaspoon salt, and ½ teaspoon pepper. Before serving, grate the apple on top and add the eggs. Pour the dressing over the salad and toss gently. Serve at room temperature.

# farro tabbouleh with feta

serves 8 to 10

*I love to take a familiar recipe and give it a twist. Instead of using bulgur wheat for this tabbouleh, I made it with farro, which is a chewier and nuttier grain, along with chickpeas, olives, and feta. As with a traditional tabbouleh, I add lots of parsley, mint, and a fresh lemon vinaigrette.*

2½ cups pearled farro (1 pound)

Kosher salt and freshly ground black pepper

2 hothouse cucumbers, unpeeled, halved, seeded, and ½-inch diced

1 (15-ounce) can chickpeas, drained and rinsed

8 scallions, green and white parts, thinly sliced diagonally

1½ cups chopped fresh parsley (2 bunches)

1 cup julienned fresh mint leaves (2 bunches)

1 cup good olive oil

½ cup freshly squeezed lemon juice (2 to 3 lemons)

12 ounces feta, ½-inch diced (not crumbled!)

¾ cup pitted Kalamata olives, drained

Rinse and drain the farro and place it in a large saucepan with 4 cups water and 2 teaspoons salt. Bring to a boil, lower the heat, cover, and simmer for about 20 minutes, until tender. Drain.

Meanwhile, combine the cucumbers, chickpeas, scallions, parsley, and mint in a very large bowl.

In a 2-cup glass measuring cup, whisk together the olive oil, lemon juice, 2 teaspoons salt, and 1 teaspoon pepper. Add the hot farro to the vegetables and herbs, pour the dressing on top, and stir to combine. Carefully stir in the feta, olives, 2 teaspoons salt, and 1 teaspoon pepper. Serve at room temperature.

**pro tip** If you add the vinaigrette to any grain salad, such as farro, while the grain is still warm, it will absorb more dressing and have more flavor than if it's cold.

**make ahead:** Prepare completely, cover, and refrigerate for up to 12 hours. Taste for seasonings (you'll need to add more lemon and salt) and serve cold or at room temperature.

# israeli vegetable salad

serves 6 for lunch, 8 as side dish

*I follow Danny Meyer, the founder of Union Square Hospitality Group, on Instagram. When he went to Israel, he posted pictures of dishes that had hummus not as a dip, but as a sauce to go with anything from salad to kebabs. He inspired this Middle Eastern vegetable salad using creamy hummus as a base and piling fresh vegetables and mint on top.*

1 (1 pound 13-ounce) can chickpeas, rinsed and drained

1 cup tahini (ground sesame paste)

1 cup freshly squeezed lemon juice (4 to 6 lemons), divided

3 tablespoons chopped garlic (9 cloves)

1½ teaspoons ground cumin

½ teaspoon Sriracha

Good olive oil

Kosher salt and freshly ground black pepper

1 large hothouse cucumber, unpeeled, halved, seeded, and ½-inch diced

2 cups heirloom cherry tomatoes, halved or quartered

1 cup (½-inch-diced) Holland red bell pepper (1 large)

¾ cup (¼-inch-diced) red onion

½ cup julienned fresh mint leaves, for garnish

Toasted pita bread, for serving

**pro tip** Get in the habit of tasting ingredients before you add them to be sure they're fresh. High fat items like olive oil and tahini can become rancid as they age.

**make ahead:** Prepare the hummus, the vegetable salad, and the lemon vinaigrette and set them all aside separately at room temperature. When ready to serve, toss the vegetables with the vinaigrette and assemble the salad.

For the hummus, place the chickpeas, tahini, ¾ cup of the lemon juice, the garlic, cumin, Sriracha, 2 tablespoons olive oil, 1 tablespoon salt, and 1 teaspoon black pepper in the bowl of a food processor fitted with the steel blade and process until the mixture is completely smooth. If the hummus is too thick, add a few tablespoons of warm water until it is creamy but still thick and spreadable.

In a large bowl, combine the cucumber, tomatoes, bell pepper, and red onion. Add ⅓ cup olive oil, the remaining ¼ cup lemon juice, 2 teaspoons salt, and 1 teaspoon black pepper and combine.

Spoon the hummus onto a large (12 × 16-inch) serving platter, spreading it out with a raised edge. With a slotted spoon, mound the vegetable salad on the hummus, leaving the edges of the hummus visible. Sprinkle the vegetables and hummus with the mint and extra salt. Drizzle with olive oil and serve at room temperature with pita bread.

# pork posole

serves 6 to 8

*Pork posole is a delicious Mexican soup/stew that's hearty enough to be an entire meal.* Posole *is the Spanish word for hominy, which is dried corn, the signature ingredient in the soup. It's particularly fun to eat because each hearty bowl of soup has avocado, scallions, Cheddar cheese, sour cream, and tortilla chips piled on top.*

**Good olive oil**

**1½ pounds lean, boneless pork loin, ½-inch diced**

**2 cups chopped yellow onion (2 onions)**

**⅓ cup small-diced poblano pepper**

**2 Holland yellow or orange bell peppers, seeded and ¾-inch diced**

**1 tablespoon minced garlic (3 cloves)**

**1 teaspoon chili powder**

**½ teaspoon dried oregano**

**6 cups good chicken stock, preferably homemade (page 259), simmering**

**1 (12-ounce) jar medium salsa verde, such as Goya**

**2 (15-ounce) cans white hominy, such as Goya, rinsed and drained**

**1 (15.5-ounce) can black beans, such as Goya, rinsed and drained**

**3 cups yellow corn tortilla chips, plus extra for serving**

**Kosher salt and freshly ground black pepper**

**Lime wedges, sliced or diced avocado, sliced scallions, sliced radishes, grated Cheddar, and sour cream, for serving**

make ahead: Reheat this (and all soups) slowly, adding extra chicken stock or water, until it is the desired thickness.

Heat 3 tablespoons olive oil in a medium (11-inch) pot or Dutch oven, such as Le Creuset, over medium-high heat. Add the pork and sauté for 5 to 10 minutes, until lightly browned on all sides. Transfer the pork and any liquid to a bowl and set aside. Heat 2 tablespoons oil in the pot, add the onions, and sauté over medium heat for 5 minutes, stirring occasionally. Add the poblano and bell peppers and cook for 5 minutes, stirring occasionally. Add the garlic, chili powder, and oregano and cook for one minute. Return the pork and its juices to the pot.

*recipe continues*

Add the chicken stock and salsa verde and bring to a simmer. Stir in the hominy, black beans, corn chips, 1 tablespoon salt, and 1½ teaspoons black pepper and simmer, partially covered, for 30 minutes, stirring occasionally. Add 1 teaspoon salt, depending on the saltiness of the chicken stock and the chips.

To serve, ladle the posole into large soup bowls. Garnish with a squeeze of lime and top with avocado, scallions, radishes, tortilla chips, Cheddar, and sour cream. Serve hot.

**pro tip** To remove an avocado from the skin without breaking it, use a large soup spoon.

# roasted beet, butternut squash & apple salad

serves 4 to 6

*A warm salad with apples, roasted beets, and squash is the perfect autumn lunch. It's both sweet and savory and I love the way the balsamic vinaigrette with its hints of orange, honey, and Dijon mustard works with the vegetables.*

**1 pound red beets, tops removed, peeled and ½-inch diced**

**Good olive oil**

**Kosher salt and freshly ground black pepper**

**1 pound butternut squash, peeled and ½-inch diced**

**1 pound crisp red apples, halved, cored, and ½-inch sliced**

**1 large shallot, halved and sliced**

**1 teaspoon minced garlic**

**2 tablespoons balsamic vinegar**

**1 teaspoon grated orange zest**

**1½ tablespoons freshly squeezed orange juice**

**1 tablespoon liquid honey**

**1½ teaspoons good Dijon mustard**

**3 ounces baby arugula (6 cups)**

**¼ cup roasted, salted Marcona almonds**

Preheat the oven to 450 degrees. Arrange two oven racks evenly spaced.

Place the beets on a sheet pan, toss with 2 tablespoons olive oil, ½ teaspoon salt, and ½ teaspoon pepper, and spread out in one layer. On a second sheet pan, toss the butternut squash and apples with 2 tablespoons olive oil, 1 teaspoon salt, and ½ teaspoon pepper and spread out in one layer. Roast both pans of vegetables for 25 to 30 minutes, tossing occasionally, until everything is tender and lightly browned.

Meanwhile, for the vinaigrette, heat ⅓ cup olive oil in a small sauté pan over medium-low heat. Add the shallot and cook for 3 minutes. Add the garlic and cook for 30 seconds. Over low heat, whisk in the balsamic vinegar, orange zest, orange juice, honey, mustard, ½ teaspoon salt, and ¼ teaspoon pepper. Keep warm.

Place the roasted vegetables and fruit in a large bowl. Add the arugula and vinaigrette and toss well. Sprinkle with the almonds and serve warm.

**pro tip** Cut the beets on a sheet of parchment paper to keep them from staining the cutting board.

# tomato & avocado salad

serves 4 to 6

*My friend Barbara Liberman made this salad for us and it was so simple and delicious that I asked her for the recipe. I love when a few simple ingredients meld together and the whole is much greater than its parts. In summer the tomatoes, avocados, onion, arugula, and lemon vinaigrette are the perfect side dish for a simple grilled chicken, steak, or ribs.*

**¼ cup plus 2 tablespoons freshly squeezed lemon juice, divided (2 lemons)**

**2 firm, ripe Hass avocados (see tip)**

**2 pints cherry or grape tomatoes, halved through the stem (see tip)**

**½ cup medium-diced red onion**

**Good olive oil**

**Kosher salt and freshly ground black pepper**

**3 ounces baby arugula**

**pro tip** Buy avocados a day or two in advance and allow them to ripen at room temperature in a paper bag just until the skins turn from green to a greenish brown color. Refrigerate ripe avocados to keep them from overripening.

Pour ¼ cup of the lemon juice into a mixing bowl. Cut the avocados in half, remove the pit, peel them (or scoop them out with a spoon), and cut in ½-inch dice. Immediately add the avocados to the lemon juice and toss carefully. Add the cherry tomatoes and red onion and toss again.

In a small glass measuring cup, whisk together the remaining 2 tablespoons of lemon juice, ¼ cup olive oil, ½ teaspoon salt, and ½ teaspoon pepper.

Pour enough of the vinaigrette over the tomato and avocado mixture to moisten completely. Add the arugula, add more vinaigrette, sprinkle with 1½ teaspoons salt and ½ teaspoon pepper, and toss well. Taste for seasonings (you want the salad well seasoned!) and serve at room temperature.

**pro tip** A small serrated knife cuts tomatoes easily without squashing them.

# tomato & eggplant soup

serves 6

*You'll find all the flavors of a good marinara sauce in this substantial soup, along with the smoky richness of roasted eggplant. As an added bonus, the leftovers can become the basis of Baked Pasta with Tomatoes & Eggplant (page 83) the next day!*

**Good olive oil**
**4½ cups (½-inch-diced) unpeeled eggplant (1 pound)**
**2 cups chopped yellow onion (2 onions)**
**2 cups chopped fennel bulb**
**2 tablespoons minced garlic (6 cloves)**
**3 cups good chicken stock, preferably homemade (page 259)**
**1 (28-ounce) can crushed tomatoes, preferably San Marzano**
**2 teaspoons whole dried fennel seeds**
**1½ teaspoons dried oregano**
**1 teaspoon fresh thyme leaves**
**¼ teaspoon crushed red pepper flakes**
**Kosher salt and freshly ground black pepper**
**1 (28-ounce) can whole peeled tomatoes, preferably San Marzano**
**Freshly grated Italian Parmesan cheese, for serving**

**pro tip** To cut eggplant and other round vegetables, first cut them in half lengthwise, then place each half flat side down on the board before you cut it. The vegetable will be more stable and easier to cut without a trip to the hospital.

**make ahead:** Pack in containers and refrigerate for up to a week or freeze for up to 4 months.

Heat ½ cup olive oil in a medium (10 to 11-inch) pot or Dutch oven, such as Le Creuset, over medium heat. Add the eggplant and sauté for 5 minutes, stirring frequently, until tender. Add a little more olive oil if the eggplant is sticking.

Add 2 tablespoons olive oil to the pot, add the onions and fennel, and cook for 6 to 8 minutes, stirring occasionally, until the onion is tender but not browned. Add the garlic and cook for one minute, stirring often. Add the chicken stock, crushed tomatoes, fennel seeds, oregano, thyme, red pepper flakes, 1 tablespoon salt, and 2 teaspoons black pepper. Pour the can of whole tomatoes, including the liquid, into a food processor and pulse until the tomatoes are coarsely chopped. Add the tomatoes and the liquid to the pot. Bring to a boil, lower the heat, and simmer uncovered for 15 minutes, stirring occasionally. Taste for seasonings. Serve hot in large bowls sprinkled with Parmesan cheese and a drizzle of olive oil.

# heirloom tomatoes
## with herbed ricotta

serves 6

*Once I learned how easy it is to make fresh ricotta, I never went back to store-bought. It makes a world of difference in simple dishes like this one. When tomatoes are in season in East Hampton, I like to do a big platter piled with a mound of ricotta mixed with scallions and dill and surrounded by lots of colorful heirloom tomatoes. I serve it family style and everyone helps themselves.*

**2 cups fresh ricotta, preferably homemade (page 264)**

**3 tablespoons minced scallions, white and green parts (2 scallions)**

**2 tablespoons minced fresh dill**

**1 tablespoon minced fresh chives**

**Kosher salt and freshly ground black pepper**

**2 pints assorted heirloom tomatoes**

**1 teaspoon minced garlic**

**1 tablespoon good olive oil, plus more for drizzling**

**½ cup julienned fresh basil leaves, plus extra for garnish**

**Fleur de sel**

In a medium bowl, combine the ricotta, scallions, dill, chives, 1 teaspoon salt, and ½ teaspoon pepper and set aside for up to 30 minutes.

With a small serrated knife, cut the larger tomatoes in wedges through the stem and the smaller tomatoes in half through the stem. Place them in a medium bowl with the garlic, olive oil, 1 teaspoon salt, and ½ teaspoon pepper and set aside.

When ready to serve, add the basil to the tomatoes and combine. Pile the ricotta in a large (12-inch) round shallow bowl or oval platter. Using a slotted spoon, place the tomatoes around the ricotta, discarding any liquid. Drizzle the tomatoes and ricotta with olive oil, sprinkle with the reserved basil and fleur de sel, and serve at room temperature.

# tricolore salad with oranges

serves 8

*This is a simple Italian salad with really interesting ingredients: radicchio, endive, arugula, oranges, and olives and a lemon vinaigrette. It's a great winter salad to serve with a roast chicken.*

1 cup shallots, peeled, thinly sliced in rings, and separated
    (2 to 4 shallots)
2 tablespoons apple cider vinegar
1 large radicchio, halved, cored, and shredded like slaw
    (12 ounces)
1 large endive, halved lengthwise, cored, and sliced crosswise
    ½ inch thick (8 ounces)
3 ounces baby arugula
4 navel oranges, peeled and sliced in ¼-inch-thick half-rounds
    (see tip)
⅔ cup pitted Kalamata olives
½ cup freshly squeezed lemon juice (2 to 3 lemons)
½ teaspoon good Dijon mustard
Kosher salt and freshly ground black pepper
½ cup good olive oil

**pro tip** For a more professional peeled orange, slice off the top and bottom, stand it upright on the board, and remove the peel by cutting along the contour of the orange, making sure to remove all the white pith.

Place the shallots in a small shallow bowl and pour the vinegar over them. Set aside for 10 minutes to macerate.

In a large shallow serving bowl, combine the radicchio, endive, arugula, oranges, and olives. Lift the shallots from the vinegar with a slotted spoon, sprinkle them on the salad, and toss lightly (discard the vinegar).

In a 1-cup glass measuring cup, whisk together the lemon juice, mustard, 1 teaspoon salt, and ½ teaspoon pepper. While whisking, slowly add the olive oil. Pour enough of the vinaigrette over the salad to moisten well. Sprinkle with one more teaspoon salt, toss well, and taste for seasonings. Serve at room temperature.

# turkey sandwiches
## with brussels sprout slaw

serves 6

*John Karangis, the wonderful executive chef at Danny Meyer's Union Square Events, invited me for lunch and made turkey sandwiches with Brussels sprout coleslaw. I thought it was such a brilliant twist on regular coleslaw that I came right home and made my own version. Sometimes I can find individual Italian ciabatta rolls, but if not, I make the sandwiches on large ciabatta loaves and cut them into individual portions.*

**12 ounces Brussels sprouts, trimmed**

**¾ cup good mayonnaise, such as Hellmann's, plus extra for spreading**

**2 tablespoons whole-grain mustard**

**1 tablespoon good Dijon mustard**

**1 tablespoon apple cider vinegar**

**Kosher salt and freshly ground black pepper**

**6 individual or 2 large ciabatta breads, halved and toasted (see tip)**

**¾ pound sliced turkey breast**

Set up a food processor with the slicing disk and process the Brussels sprouts through the feed tube. (You don't need to remove the cores of the sprouts.) Transfer to a large bowl.

In a medium bowl, whisk together the mayonnaise, whole-grain mustard, Dijon mustard, vinegar, 1 teaspoon salt, and ½ teaspoon pepper. Add the mayonnaise mixture to the sprouts and toss well.

Place the ciabatta halves, cut sides up, on a cutting board. Spread a thin layer of mayonnaise over each half. Place a layer of turkey on the bottom halves, pile some of the slaw on top, and place a second layer of turkey on top of the slaw. Sprinkle generously with salt and pepper. Cover with the top halves of the breads, cut sides down. Serve the individual ciabattas cut in half or cut the large ciabattas in thirds and serve.

**pro tip** To toast the bread in the oven, place the bread, cut side up, on a sheet pan and bake them at 350 degrees for 10 to 15 minutes.

**make ahead:** You can prepare the slaw up to 6 hours ahead and refrigerate. Assemble the sandwiches just before serving.

# tuscan tomato & bread salad

serves 6 to 8

*The first time my assistant Barbara and I made panzanella, an Italian bread salad, we ate all the vinaigrette-soaked bread first, laughed, then finally ate the vegetables. This salad is a mash-up of Caprese salad and panzanella. I think it's the best of both worlds!*

1 pound cherry or grape tomatoes, halved through the stem

1 pound fresh mozzarella, ¾-inch diced

2 teaspoons minced garlic (2 cloves)

1 teaspoon good Dijon mustard

¼ cup good red wine vinegar

Kosher salt and freshly ground black pepper

½ cup plus ⅓ cup good olive oil

½ pound sourdough bread, crusts removed and ¾-inch diced

20 fresh basil leaves, julienned

**pro tip** You can use tongs to turn the bread cubes so they brown evenly or you can toss them by holding the handle of the pan and flipping the croutons in a C motion away from you.

Place the tomatoes and mozzarella in a large bowl. Put the garlic, mustard, vinegar, ½ teaspoon salt, and ¼ teaspoon pepper in a 1-cup glass measuring cup and slowly whisk in the ½ cup of olive oil. Set aside.

Heat the remaining ⅓ cup of olive oil in a large (12-inch) sauté pan until hot but not smoking. Add the bread cubes and sprinkle with 1 teaspoon salt and ½ teaspoon pepper. Sauté over medium to medium-high heat for 5 to 8 minutes, tossing occasionally, until the bread is evenly browned and crisp. Add the warm bread to the tomatoes and mozzarella. Add enough of the vinaigrette to moisten all the ingredients. Add the basil, sprinkle with salt and pepper, and toss carefully, adding more vinaigrette if necessary. Serve at room temperature.

# filet of beef carpaccio

serves 6 to 8

*I think raw beef carpaccio is a little boring. Searing the beef briefly and adding a drizzle of Caesar dressing makes it so much more flavorful.*

1¼ pounds filet of beef, trimmed and tied

¾ cup good olive oil, plus extra for the beef

Kosher salt and freshly ground black pepper

2 extra-large egg yolks, at room temperature

2 teaspoons good Dijon mustard, at room temperature

1 tablespoon chopped garlic (3 cloves)

2 anchovy fillets, drained

½ cup freshly squeezed lemon juice, at room temperature
   (2 to 3 lemons)

¼ cup canola oil

½ cup freshly grated Italian Parmesan cheese, plus shaved
   Parmesan for garnish (see tip, page 46)

2 tablespoons capers, drained

3 cups baby arugula

Flaked sea salt, such as Maldon, for sprinkling

Rub the beef with olive oil and sprinkle all over with 2 teaspoons kosher salt and 1 teaspoon freshly ground black pepper. Heat a sauté pan over high heat and sear the filet on all sides, turning it with tongs. Wrap the beef in plastic wrap and freeze for 2 hours, turning once to freeze evenly.

Meanwhile, place the egg yolks, mustard, garlic, anchovies, lemon juice, 2½ teaspoons kosher salt, and 1 teaspoon pepper in a food processor fitted with the steel blade and process for 15 seconds. Combine the ¾ cup olive oil and the canola oil in a glass measuring cup. With the food processor running, slowly pour the oils down the feed tube in a thin stream. Add the grated Parmesan and pulse to combine.

Remove the string from the beef and slice it very thin with a sharp slicing or smoked salmon knife. Place 5 slices on each dinner plate in a single layer. Drizzle the beef generously with the dressing and (in this order) sprinkle with the capers, kosher salt, pepper, arugula, shaved Parmesan, and sea salt. Serve at room temperature with a pitcher of extra dressing on the side.

**pro tip** Since you're slicing this by hand, it will never be paper thin, but freezing it makes it so much easier. Just slice it as thinly as possible and it will be delicious.

**pro tip** Be sure to choose a really good-quality Italian Parmesan for this recipe; it makes all the difference.

# cauliflower toasts

serves 6

*Cauliflower is, in my opinion, a highly underappreciated vegetable. Roasting brings out its flavor. Lots of Gruyère and prosciutto add flavor and texture.*

1 small head cauliflower (2 pounds)

4 tablespoons good olive oil

¼ teaspoon crushed red pepper flakes

Kosher salt and freshly ground black pepper

12 ounces Italian mascarpone cheese, at room temperature

6 ounces Gruyère cheese, grated

4 ounces thinly sliced prosciutto, julienned

¼ teaspoon ground nutmeg

6 large slices country-style bread

Paprika

Freshly grated Italian Parmesan cheese

2 tablespoons minced fresh chives

Flaked sea salt, such as Maldon

**pro tip** Always cut cauliflower from the stem end, not the top. You'll keep the florets intact and avoid getting cauliflower crumbles all over your counter.

Preheat the oven to 400 degrees.

Turn the cauliflower upside down on a cutting board. Cut off and discard most but not all of the stems, then cut the florets into small, ½-inch clusters. Place the florets on a sheet pan, toss them with the olive oil, red pepper flakes, 1 teaspoon salt, and ½ teaspoon black pepper, and spread them out in a single layer. Roast for 25 to 30 minutes, tossing two or three times, until the florets are tender and randomly browned. Set aside to cool for 10 minutes.

Set the oven to broil and arrange a rack 6 inches below the heat.

Transfer the florets to a large mixing bowl and add the mascarpone, stirring to coat the florets evenly. Stir in the Gruyère, prosciutto, nutmeg, 1 teaspoon salt, and ½ teaspoon black pepper.

Toast the bread in a toaster until lightly browned, and place in a single layer on a sheet pan lined with foil. Mound the cauliflower mixture evenly on each toast and dust with paprika. Broil the toasts for 2 to 4 minutes, until browned and bubbling. (Watch them carefully!) Transfer to plates and sprinkle with Parmesan, the chives, and sea salt. Serve hot.

dinner

# is it done yet??

Part of the challenge of cooking is not just preparing the roast or mixing up the cake batter but also knowing when they're perfectly cooked. We've all stood over a charcoal grill blankly staring at the steak and wondering, "Is it done yet?" You can start with the most delicious ingredients in the world, but if you overcook the lamb or underbake the muffins, you're in trouble!

For baking, the tests are fairly straightforward and the same for almost all cakes. First, lightly press the rounded top of the cake. Does your finger make a mark or does the cake bounce back? If it bounces back, it's probably done. Next, insert a toothpick into the center of the cake. If the skewer comes out clean or with just a crumb or two attached, the cake is done. If you're testing a cake that has ingredients like chocolate in the batter, you should test the cake in several places; if you hit a puddle of molten chocolate your skewer might come out wet even when the cake is done.

Testing meat is a little more complicated because its temperature will continue to rise during the resting period, as much as 5 to 10 degrees, depending on the size of the piece of meat. (Larger roasts like standing rib roasts hold more heat and will continue to cook longer.) To make sure the meat doesn't go past the target temperature after it rests,

you need to take it out of the oven (or off the grill) a little before it's done. That's why in my recipes the recommended internal temperatures indicate the temperature you want *before* the meat rests under foil. See page 268 for a chart of target temperatures for the most common meats and poultry.

Seafood is generally judged for doneness by a visual test. Cooked fish will flake easily with a fork when it's done, and shrimp will be just firm and pink. The exception is lobster, which should reach 140 degrees when tested in the tail with an instant-read thermometer. And for all cooked pasta you want it to be al dente, or "to the tooth," when it's done, which means that it's cooked through but gives a little resistance when you bite into it. Use the recommended timing on the package as a loose guideline and start testing it 2 minutes before that timing to make sure it doesn't overcook.

LONG RING TIMERS

INSTANT-READ THERMOMETERS FOR MEATS

WOODEN SKEWERS FOR CAKE TESTERS

PAIRING KNIVES FOR TESTING DONENESS OF VEGETABLES

# baked pasta
## with tomatoes & eggplant

serves 3

*I love what I call two-fers. I don't love reheating something I served for dinner a second day, but with two-fers, the leftovers become something totally different. This is one of those recipes: you make the Tomato & Eggplant Soup (page 62) for dinner one night and use the leftover soup as a pasta sauce the next.*

**Kosher salt and freshly ground black pepper**
**8 ounces penne rigate and/or fusilli**
**3 cups Tomato & Eggplant Soup (page 62)**
**4 ounces fresh mozzarella, medium-diced**
**5 tablespoons freshly grated Italian Parmesan cheese, divided**
**2 tablespoons unsalted butter, small-diced**

Preheat the oven to 500 degrees. (Make sure your oven is clean!) Place three (6-inch) gratin dishes on a sheet pan and set aside.

Boil a large pot of water, add a tablespoon of salt, and add the pasta. If you're using one type of pasta, cook it for 1 to 2 minutes less than the directions on the package. If you're using two kinds of pasta, start with the one that cooks longest and add the second later so they finish at the same time. You want the pasta to be quite al dente. Drain.

Pour the soup into a large bowl, add the cooked pasta, the mozzarella, 2 tablespoons of the Parmesan, 1½ teaspoons salt, and ¾ teaspoon pepper and toss well. Divide the mixture evenly among the three gratin dishes, dot the tops with the butter, and bake for 10 minutes, until hot and bubbly and the pasta begins to brown. Sprinkle each dish with 1 tablespoon of the remaining Parmesan, bake for another 4 minutes, and serve hot.

**pro tip** Of course, you can bake this pasta in one larger dish; but making individual gratins looks so much more professional!

**pro tip** I love using two different kinds of pasta, not only because they add great texture but because you use up the leftover boxes of pasta in your pantry.

# chicken marbella, updated

serves 6

*Nora Ephron once commented that in the 1980s whenever you went to a dinner party in New York City, everyone served Chicken Marbella, from* The Silver Palate Cookbook. *This chicken is marinated with prunes, olives, capers, and a stunning amount of garlic. There's a reason it was so popular; it's full of big flavors and is so easy to make. I revisited the old recipe, tweaking the flavors a little, and it's better than ever!*

½ cup good olive oil
½ cup good red wine vinegar
1½ cups large pitted prunes, such as Sunsweet
1 cup large green olives, pitted, such as Cerignola (see tip)
½ cup capers, including the juices (3½ ounces)
6 bay leaves
1½ heads of garlic, cloves separated, peeled, and minced (see tip)
¼ cup dried oregano
Kosher salt and freshly ground black pepper
2 (4-pound) chickens, backs removed and cut in 8 pieces
½ cup light brown sugar, lightly packed
1 cup dry white wine, such as Pinot Grigio

**pro tip** You can't buy good-quality pitted green olives. I buy whole olives and pit them with a cherry pitter.

**pro tip** To peel a lot of garlic quickly, separate the cloves and blanch them in boiling water for 15 to 30 seconds, depending on the size of the cloves—the peel slips right off.

Combine the olive oil, vinegar, prunes, olives, capers, bay leaves, garlic, oregano, 2 tablespoons salt, and 2 teaspoons pepper in a large bowl. Add the chicken to the marinade. (You can also place the chicken and marinade in a 2-gallon plastic storage bag and squeeze out the air to make sure the chicken is fully covered with the marinade.) Refrigerate overnight, turning occasionally to be sure the marinade is getting into all of the chicken pieces.

Preheat the oven to 350 degrees.

Place the chicken, skin side up, along with the marinade in one layer in a large (15 × 18-inch) roasting pan, sprinkle with the brown sugar, 2 teaspoons salt, and 1 teaspoon pepper, and pour the wine around *(not over!)* the chicken. Roast for 45 to 55 minutes, until the internal temperature of the chicken is 145 degrees. Remove the pan from the oven, cover tightly with aluminum foil, and allow to rest for 10 to 15 minutes. Discard the bay leaves. Transfer the chicken, prunes, and olives to a serving platter, sprinkle with salt, and serve hot with the pan juices.

# cioppino

serves 6

*Cioppino is a seafood stew that was created by Italian immigrant fishermen in San Francisco in the late 1800s. Whenever a fisherman came home empty-handed, he would bring a pot around to his neighbors and they would share part of their day's catch with him so he could make soup for his family. There are lots of variations of cioppino, but mine has cod, shrimp, scallops, and mussels, along with lots of vegetables and herbs to make it really flavorful.*

Good olive oil

2 cups (½-inch-diced) fennel bulb

1½ cups (½-inch-diced) yellow onion (1 large)

1 tablespoon minced garlic (3 cloves)

1 teaspoon whole dried fennel seeds

½ teaspoon crushed red pepper flakes

1 (28-ounce) can crushed tomatoes, such as San Marzano

4 cups seafood stock, preferably homemade (page 261)

1½ cups dry white wine, such as Pinot Grigio

Kosher salt and freshly ground black pepper

1½ pounds center-cut cod fillets, skin removed, 2-inch diced

1 pound large (16 to 20-count) shrimp, peeled and deveined

1 pound sea scallops, halved crosswise

24 mussels, scrubbed (see tip)

1 tablespoon Pernod

3 tablespoons minced fresh parsley

Garlic Toasts (recipe follows), for serving

Heat ¼ cup olive oil in a large (12-inch) heavy pot or Dutch oven, such as Le Creuset, over medium heat. Add the fennel and onion and sauté for 10 minutes, until tender. Stir in the garlic, fennel seeds, and red pepper flakes and cook for 2 minutes, until fragrant. Add the tomatoes, stock, wine, 1 tablespoon salt, and 1 teaspoon black pepper. Bring to a boil, lower the heat, and simmer uncovered for 30 minutes. The stock will be highly seasoned.

**pro tip** Scrub mussels with a wire brush, then soak them in water with a few tablespoons of flour for 30 minutes. This will help them disgorge any sand. Rinse the mussels before using.

**make ahead:** Prepare the soup base up to 2 days ahead and refrigerate. Reheat and add the seafood just before serving.

*recipe continues*

Add the seafood in the following order: first the cod, then the shrimp, scallops, and finally the mussels. Do not stir! Bring to a simmer, lower the heat, cover, and cook for 8 to 10 minutes, until all the seafood is cooked and the mussels are open. Stir in the Pernod, being careful not to break up the fish; cover and set aside for 3 minutes for the flavors to blend. Discard any mussels that have not opened. Ladle into large shallow bowls, sprinkle with parsley, and serve hot with garlic toasts.

# garlic toasts

makes 20 to 25 toasts

**1 baguette**
**¼ cup good olive oil**
**Kosher salt and freshly ground black pepper**
**1 garlic clove, halved lengthwise**

Preheat the oven to 400 degrees.

Slice the baguette diagonally in ¼-inch-thick slices. Depending on the size of the baguette, you should get 20 to 25 slices.

Lay the slices in one layer on a sheet pan, brush each with olive oil, and sprinkle generously with salt and pepper. Bake for 15 to 20 minutes, until browned and crisp. As soon as they're cool enough to handle, rub the top of the toasts with a cut side of the garlic. Serve at room temperature.

# chicken thighs
## with creamy mustard sauce

serves 4

*I like doing the high-low thing: taking an inexpensive cut of meat like chicken thighs and serving it with a rich, flavorful sauce made with white wine, crème fraîche, and lots of mustard. It's also fun to serve it in a casual way by placing the skillet in the middle of the table and letting everyone help themselves.*

**8 medium bone-in, skin-on chicken thighs (2¼ pounds)**

**Kosher salt and freshly ground black pepper**

**Good olive oil**

**2 cups halved and thinly sliced yellow onion (2 onions)**

**2 tablespoons dry white wine**

**8 ounces crème fraîche**

**1 tablespoon good Dijon mustard**

**1 teaspoon whole-grain mustard**

**1 tablespoon chopped fresh parsley**

Place the chicken thighs on a cutting board, skin side up, and pat them dry with paper towels. Sprinkle the chicken with 1½ teaspoons salt and ¾ teaspoon pepper. Turn them over and sprinkle them with one more teaspoon of salt.

 **pro tip** To ensure the chicken cooks evenly, choose thighs that are similar in size.

Heat 1 tablespoon olive oil in a large (11 to 12-inch) cast-iron skillet over medium heat. When the oil is hot, place the chicken in the pan in one layer, skin side down. Cook over medium heat for 15 minutes without moving, until the skin is golden brown. (If the skin gets too dark, turn the heat to medium low.) Turn the chicken pieces with tongs, add the onions to the pan, including under the chicken, and cook over medium heat for 15 minutes, stirring the onions occasionally, until the thighs are cooked to 155 to 160 degrees and the onions are browned. Transfer the chicken (not the onions) to a plate and allow to rest uncovered while you make the sauce. If the onions aren't browned, cook them for another minute.

Add the wine, crème fraîche, Dijon mustard, whole-grain mustard, and 1 teaspoon salt to the skillet and stir over medium heat for one minute. Return the chicken, skin side up, and the juices to the skillet, sprinkle with parsley, and serve hot.

# crispy mustard chicken & frisée

serves 4

*This is a great summer dinner! I love the interplay of hot and cold—the crispy chicken and roasted fingerling potatoes with the slightly bitter greens and mustard vinaigrette. This hits all the right notes for me.*

**2 garlic cloves**

**1½ teaspoons fresh thyme leaves**

**Kosher salt and freshly ground black pepper**

**1 cup panko (Japanese bread flakes)**

**1½ teaspoons grated lemon zest**

**Good olive oil**

**1 tablespoon unsalted butter, melted**

**¼ cup good Dijon mustard**

**¼ cup dry white wine**

**1½ pounds bone-in, skin-on chicken thighs (4 large)**

**1 pound fingerling potatoes, halved lengthwise**

**12 ounces baby frisée or chicory salad greens (see tip)**

**Mustard Vinaigrette (recipe follows)**

Preheat the oven to 375 degrees.

Place the garlic, thyme, 1 teaspoon salt, and ½ teaspoon pepper in a food processor fitted with the steel blade and process until the garlic is finely minced. Add the panko, lemon zest, 1 tablespoon olive oil, and the butter and pulse a few times to moisten the panko. Pour the mixture into a shallow bowl. In another shallow bowl, whisk together the mustard and wine.

Pat the chicken thighs dry with paper towels and sprinkle generously with salt and pepper. Dip each piece first in the mustard mixture to coat the top and bottom and then coat the skin side *only* in the crumb mixture, pressing gently to make the crumbs adhere. Place the chicken on one side of a sheet pan, crumb side up, and press any remaining crumbs onto the chicken.

Place the potatoes, 1 tablespoon olive oil, 1 teaspoon salt, and ½ teaspoon pepper in a bowl and toss. Spread the potatoes on the

**pro tip** Vinaigrette won't cling to wet lettuce. Wash and thoroughly spin-dry greens before dressing them.

*recipe continues*

other side of the sheet pan in one layer and roast both together for 40 to 50 minutes, turning the potatoes once during roasting, until the chicken reaches an internal temperature of 160 degrees. The chicken and potatoes should be done at the same time.

Meanwhile, place the greens on a serving platter. When the chicken and potatoes are done, toss the salad with enough vinaigrette to moisten and place the chicken and potatoes on top, adding any crumbs from the sheet pan. Sprinkle with salt and serve while the chicken and potatoes are still warm.

# mustard vinaigrette

makes ¾ cup

**¼ cup minced shallots**
**¼ cup apple cider vinegar**
**½ cup good olive oil**
**1 tablespoon good Dijon mustard**
**Kosher salt and freshly ground black pepper**

Place the shallots, vinegar, olive oil, mustard, 1 teaspoon salt, and ½ teaspoon pepper in a small bowl and whisk until emulsified.

**pro tip** To cut onions or shallots neatly, cut them in half and peel them, leaving the root end intact before slicing, chopping, or mincing. Otherwise, you'll have onions all over your cutting board!

# filet of beef
## with mushrooms & blue cheese

serves 4 to 6

*I love to roast a filet of beef for the holidays, because it's so simple and yet so special. While the filet is roasting, I make a luxurious sauce with shallots, wild mushrooms, Roquefort cheese, Port wine, and lots of crème fraîche.*

2½ pounds beef tenderloin, trimmed and tied

7 tablespoons unsalted butter, at room temperature, divided

Kosher salt and freshly ground black pepper

¾ cup chopped shallots (3 large)

14 ounces mushrooms, such as cremini and/or shiitakes, stems discarded and caps sliced ¼ inch thick

½ cup ruby Port wine, such as Sandeman

¾ cup crème fraîche

3 ounces Roquefort, or other strong blue cheese, crumbled

1 tablespoon minced fresh parsley

**pro tip** Tying the filet of beef ensures that it's a uniform thickness that will cook evenly. Because the thickness of the meat is the same, both a whole or half beef tenderloin cook in exactly the same amount of time, so if you double the recipe for a crowd, there's no need to adjust the cooking time.

**pro tip** Before setting your oven to 500 degrees make sure it's clean, so you don't smoke up your kitchen!

Preheat the oven to 500 degrees. Line a sheet pan with aluminum foil.

Place the beef on the prepared sheet pan and pat dry with paper towels. Spread 1 tablespoon of the butter all over the beef with your hands. Sprinkle the beef all over with 1½ teaspoons salt and 1 teaspoon pepper. Roast for exactly 25 minutes for rare (120 degrees) and 30 minutes for medium rare (125 degrees). Remove the beef from the oven, cover tightly with aluminum foil, and allow to rest for 20 minutes.

Meanwhile, make the sauce. Heat 2 tablespoons of the butter in a large (12-inch) sauté pan. Add the shallots and sauté over medium heat for 3 to 4 minutes, until tender but not browned. Add the remaining 4 tablespoons of butter and heat until sizzling. Add the mushrooms and sauté, stirring frequently, for 5 to 7 minutes, until lightly browned. Add the Port, 1 teaspoon salt, and ½ teaspoon pepper and cook for 2 to 3 minutes. Add the crème fraîche and cook for one minute, until slightly thickened. Reduce the heat to low and add the Roquefort, stirring just until it melts. (If the sauce is too thick, add another splash of Port.)

Before serving, reheat the sauce and sprinkle with the parsley. Remove the strings from the roast and slice thickly. Spoon on the sauce, sprinkle with salt, and serve hot.

# flounder milanese

serves 6

*One of my all-time favorite dinners is the Parmesan Chicken in Barefoot Contessa Family Style. It's easy and it's a whole meal on one plate. I tried the same technique with flounder and found that the warm, flaky fish with the cold arugula salad and lemon vinaigrette are amazing together!*

> 6 flounder or sole fillets (1¾ pounds total)
> 1 cup all-purpose flour
> Kosher salt and freshly ground black pepper
> 2 extra-large eggs
> 1¼ cups seasoned dry bread crumbs, such as Progresso
> Unsalted butter
> Good olive oil
> 6 ounces arugula or mixed salad greens for 6
> Lemon Vinaigrette (recipe follows)
> 2 tablespoons drained capers
> Freshly grated Italian Parmesan cheese, lemon juice, and
>      fleur de sel, for serving

Preheat the oven to 250 degrees and place a sheet pan in the oven.

Dry the fish on both sides with paper towels. Combine the flour, 2 teaspoons salt, and 1 teaspoon pepper on a dinner plate. In a low, shallow bowl, whisk the eggs with 1 tablespoon water. Put the bread crumbs on another plate. Dredge the fish on both sides in the seasoned flour and dust off the excess. Dip both sides into the egg mixture and, finally, dredge both sides in the bread crumbs.

Heat 1 tablespoon butter and 1 tablespoon olive oil in a large (12-inch) sauté pan and cook 2 fillets at a time over medium to medium-high heat for 2 to 3 minutes on each side, until cooked through. Transfer the fish in one layer to the sheet pan in the oven. Add more butter and oil and cook the rest of the fillets, transferring them to the sheet pan as they're done. Toss the arugula with enough lemon vinaigrette to moisten. Place one fillet on each plate and pile the arugula salad on top. Heat the capers in the sauté pan for 30 seconds and sprinkle over the fish and salad. Sprinkle with grated Parmesan, a squeeze of lemon juice, and the fleur de sel. Serve hot.

# lemon vinaigrette

makes ¾ cup

**¼ cup freshly squeezed lemon juice**
**½ cup good olive oil**
**Kosher salt and freshly ground black pepper**

In a small bowl or measuring cup, whisk together the lemon juice, olive oil, 1 teaspoon salt, and ½ teaspoon pepper.

**pro tip** Making vinaigrettes in a measuring cup allows you to measure and whisk at the same time.

# buttermilk herb mayo

makes 1 cup

**1 cup good mayonnaise, such as Hellmann's**
**2 tablespoons buttermilk, shaken**
**1 teaspoon good white wine vinegar**
**2 tablespoons thinly sliced scallions, white and green parts**
**1 tablespoon minced fresh parsley**
**1 tablespoon minced fresh chives**
**⅛ teaspoon minced fresh thyme leaves**
**Kosher salt and freshly ground black pepper**

Whisk together the mayonnaise, buttermilk, vinegar, scallions, parsley, chives, thyme, ½ teaspoon salt, and ¼ teaspoon pepper in a medium bowl. Cover and refrigerate until ready to use.

**pro tip** Freshly ground black pepper is an important seasoning. Instead of buying ground black pepper, I use a pepper mill and grind it myself. You can really taste the difference.

# fried chicken sandwiches

serves 6

*I was feeling cranky one day so Jeffrey took me to Shake Shack for what was then their new Chick'n Shack sandwich—a fried chicken fillet on a potato bun with buttermilk herb mayonnaise. OMG. I was thrilled when their Shake Shack cookbook came out, and I could make their sandwiches at home.*

2 cups buttermilk, shaken

1 shallot, peeled, halved lengthwise, and thinly sliced crosswise

2 garlic cloves, smashed

1 jalapeño pepper (with seeds), halved lengthwise

Kosher salt and freshly ground black pepper

3 small skinless, boneless chicken breasts (6 ounces each)

3½ cups all-purpose flour

4 teaspoons baking powder

2½ teaspoons smoked Spanish paprika

1 teaspoon cayenne pepper

1 teaspoon celery salt

2 (48-ounce) bottles canola oil

6 potato hamburger buns, toasted, for serving (see note)

Buttermilk Herb Mayo (page 102), for serving

6 Bibb lettuce leaves

Kosher dill pickles, such as Claussen, thinly sliced, for serving

Toast the buns by spreading them out, cut sides down, on a sheet pan and bake at 300 degrees for 10 to 12 minutes.

In a large bowl, whisk together the buttermilk, shallot, garlic, jalapeño, 2 teaspoons kosher salt, and 1 teaspoon black pepper. Place the chicken breasts between 2 pieces of parchment paper and, with a rolling pin or a meat mallet, pound them until they are evenly ½ inch thick. Slice each piece of chicken in half crosswise so you have 2 pieces approximately the same size. Place the chicken in the marinade, making sure each piece is well coated, cover with plastic wrap, and refrigerate for at least 8 hours or up to (but not more than) 24 hours.

When ready to cook the chicken, preheat the oven to 300 degrees. Set a wire rack on a sheet pan and place them in the oven.

In a large bowl, whisk together the flour, baking powder, paprika, cayenne pepper, celery salt, 1 tablespoon kosher salt, and 1½ teaspoons black pepper and set aside.

**pro tip** A wire strainer with a long handle is even safer than a slotted spoon for removing food from hot oil when frying. You can find them in restaurant supply stores.

*recipe continues*

Pour oil into a medium (9-inch round × 4½-inch high) Dutch oven, such as Le Creuset, until it is 2 inches deep. Clip on a candy thermometer and heat the oil over high heat until it reaches 350 degrees. Meanwhile, lift the chicken from the marinade, dredge it in the flour mixture, submerge it *again* in the marinade, then *again* in the flour mixture, lightly shaking off the excess. Transfer the chicken to a plate or sheet pan until ready to fry.

When the oil is 350 degrees, carefully lower 3 pieces *only* into the oil with tongs and adjust the heat to keep the oil at 350 degrees. Don't crowd the chicken! Cook for 5 minutes, turning once to brown evenly. With a slotted spoon, transfer the chicken to the sheet pan in the oven to keep warm. Repeat with the remaining chicken. Sprinkle all the chicken with salt and keep warm for up to 15 minutes, until ready to serve.

To assemble, place the bottom of each bun on a plate, spread with some of the buttermilk herb mayo, then a lettuce leaf, 4 pickle slices, then a piece of chicken. Spread the underside of the top bun generously with more of the mayo and place on top of the chicken, mayo side down. Serve while the chicken is still warm.

**pro tip** Cut the flat end of the garlic clove off before smashing it with the side of your knife. The peel will be easier to remove.

# 1770 house lamb & chickpea curry

serves 8

*One cold winter night, I ordered this lamb and chickpea curry at 1770 House in East Hampton. It was so delicious that I asked chef Michael Rozzi if he would share the recipe. Don't let the long list of ingredients scare you; it's not difficult and the flavors are so complex and interesting with curry, harissa, ginger, maple syrup, and coconut milk; it's really worth the time.*

2 pounds boneless lamb shoulder (not tied), gristle and fat
    removed, and 1-inch diced

¼ cup Madras curry powder

1 teaspoon ground paprika

1 teaspoon ground cumin

1 teaspoon roughly minced fresh rosemary leaves

1 teaspoon roughly minced fresh thyme leaves

½ teaspoon ground fennel seeds (see tip, page 110)

Kosher salt and freshly ground black pepper

½ cup good olive oil

1 cup chopped yellow onion

1 tablespoon chopped fresh ginger

2 teaspoons minced garlic (2 cloves)

2 cups chicken stock (page 259), or vegetable stock (page 258),
    both preferably homemade

1 (13.5-ounce) can coconut milk

½ cup dry white wine

½ cup tomato paste (6 ounces)

½ cup dark brown sugar, lightly packed

3 tablespoons pure maple syrup

2 tablespoons harissa (see note)

1 cup (¾-inch-diced) carrots (4 carrots)

1 cup (¾-inch-diced) celery (2 large stalks)

½ cup golden raisins

4 cups canned chickpeas, rinsed and drained (45 ounces)

Perfect Basmati Rice (page 160) or steamed basmati rice

Plain whole milk Greek yogurt, for serving

Whole fresh parsley or cilantro leaves, for serving

Harissa is a hot chile paste used in North African cooking. It comes in a tube and is available in the international section of your grocery store.

make ahead: Prepare the entire dish, refrigerate, and reheat slowly on top of the stove.

*recipe continues*

**pro tip** Spices are fresher when you grind them yourself. I keep a small coffee grinder in the spice drawer for grinding spices.

Place the cubed lamb in a large bowl. In a medium bowl, combine the curry powder, paprika, cumin, rosemary, thyme, fennel, 2 tablespoons salt, and 1 teaspoon pepper. Add the seasonings to the lamb, toss well to coat, and set aside for 15 to 30 minutes.

Meanwhile, heat the oil in a large (11-inch) Dutch oven, such as Le Creuset, over medium heat. Add the onion and ginger and sauté for 5 minutes, until the onion is translucent. Add the garlic and cook for one minute. Raise the heat to medium high, add the lamb and all the seasonings in the bowl, and sauté for 10 to 15 minutes, stirring occasionally, until the lamb is evenly browned. Add the chicken stock, coconut milk, wine, tomato paste, brown sugar, maple syrup, and harissa. Bring to a boil, lower the heat, and simmer, partially covered, for 1 hour, stirring occasionally.

Add the carrots, celery, raisins, chickpeas, and 2 teaspoons salt, bring to a boil, lower the heat, and simmer, partially covered, for another 30 minutes. Serve hot in shallow bowls with the rice, a dollop of yogurt, and a sprinkling of parsley.

# panko-crusted rack of lamb

serves 6

*This is the most surprising way I've made rack of lamb. It's not obvious to pair lamb with goat cheese, but the creamy goat cheese with the crunchy panko crumbs, garlic, and rosemary is absolutely delicious.*

**pro tip** "Frenched" lamb chops look more elegant. When you ask your butcher to french the lamb, he will trim the excess fat from the bones.

**4 ounces creamy goat cheese, such as Montrachet**

**1¼ cups panko (Japanese bread flakes)**

**1 tablespoon minced garlic (3 cloves)**

**1 tablespoon minced fresh rosemary leaves**

**2 teaspoons minced fresh thyme leaves**

**Fleur de sel or sea salt and freshly ground black pepper**

**Good olive oil**

**2 racks of lamb (1½ pounds each), trimmed and frenched (see tip)**

**3 tablespoons good Dijon mustard**

Preheat the oven to 450 degrees. Line a sheet pan with aluminum foil.

In a medium bowl, crumble the goat cheese with a fork. Add the panko, garlic, rosemary, thyme, 1 teaspoon fleur de sel, and 1 teaspoon pepper. Drizzle with 3 tablespoons olive oil and stir to moisten the crumbs. Set aside for a few minutes or cover and refrigerate.

Remove the racks of lamb from the refrigerator 30 minutes before you plan to cook them. Place the lamb, fat side up, on the prepared pan. Sprinkle with 2 teaspoons fleur de sel and 1 teaspoon pepper. Roast for 12 minutes exactly. Remove from the oven and, working quickly, use a knife to spread the mustard on the top of the lamb. Spread the crumb mixture evenly on the mustard, pressing gently to help the mixture adhere. Return the lamb to the oven right away and continue roasting for another 12 to 18 minutes (depending on the size of the lamb), until the crumbs are golden brown and the meat is 120 degrees for rare or 125 degrees for medium rare. (Insert an instant-read thermometer horizontally through the meat.)

Cover loosely with aluminum foil and allow the lamb to rest for 8 minutes. Cut the racks into single or double chops and serve hot.

# pork souvlaki with radish tzatziki

makes 6 souvlaki; serves 4 to 6

*Greek souvlaki is classic street food usually made with grilled skewers of lamb or chicken served in a pita bread. Instead of firing up the grill, I cook cubes of pork in a cast-iron skillet with fresh vegetables, lemon, and garlic. The radish tzatziki that I serve with it is a spicy twist on the traditional Greek cucumber yogurt sauce.*

2 pounds boneless pork shoulder, trimmed, ¾-inch diced

1 red onion, cut in ½-inch wedges through the root end

1 large Holland yellow bell pepper, seeded and cut in ½-inch strips

Grated zest of 1 lemon (see tip)

⅓ cup freshly squeezed lemon juice (2 lemons), plus extra

Good olive oil

3 garlic cloves, grated on a Microplane zester

2 tablespoons roughly chopped fresh oregano leaves

2 teaspoons roughly chopped fresh rosemary leaves

Kosher salt and freshly ground black pepper

6 warmed pita breads, for serving (see note)

Radish Tzatziki (recipe follows), for serving

Julienned fresh mint leaves, for serving

Combine the pork, red onion, bell pepper, lemon zest, lemon juice, ⅓ cup olive oil, garlic, oregano, rosemary, 2 teaspoons salt, and 1 teaspoon black pepper in a large (1-gallon) plastic storage bag. Press out the air, seal, and set aside at room temperature for 30 minutes or refrigerate for up to 12 hours.

Preheat one very large (14-inch) or two medium (10-inch) dry cast-iron skillets over high heat for 3 minutes. Add the pork and vegetables, including the marinade, spread out, and cook without stirring for 3 minutes. Continue to cook over high heat for 7 to 8 minutes, stirring occasionally, until the pork is cooked through but still slightly pink in the middle. Don't overcook the pork or it will be dry!

Place 1 warmed pita on each plate. Spoon the pork and vegetables on one half of the pita and place 2 rounded tablespoons of tzatziki on the other half. Sprinkle with mint, lemon juice, and salt and serve hot.

**pro tip** It's impossible to zest a juiced lemon, lime, or orange. Remember to zest them before you juice them.

**Warm the pitas in a 350-degree oven for 5 to 10 minutes.**

# radish tzatziki

about 1 pint

**pro tip** Grating garlic on a Microplane zester is faster and makes finer pieces of garlic, which is important because the garlic is raw in this recipe.

**6 medium radishes, scrubbed and trimmed**

**2 garlic cloves, grated on a Microplane zester**

**1¼ cups plain whole milk Greek yogurt (10 ounces)**

**1 tablespoon good olive oil**

**1 tablespoon freshly squeezed lemon juice**

**¼ cup minced scallions, white and green parts (2 scallions)**

**2½ tablespoons julienned fresh mint leaves**

**Kosher salt and freshly ground black pepper**

Grate the radishes on a box grater. Place the radishes in a paper towel and squeeze out the liquid. In a medium bowl, combine the radishes, garlic, yogurt, olive oil, lemon juice, scallions, mint, 1½ teaspoons salt, and ¾ teaspoon pepper. Cover, and refrigerate for at least 30 minutes or for up to 12 hours.

# red wine–braised short ribs

serves 6

*This may be my favorite recipe ever. In the winter when it's really cold, a hearty stew of beef short ribs simmered with a whole bottle of red wine, a bottle of Guinness, and lots of vegetables, then served over Creamy Blue Cheese Grits (page 151) or Celery Root & Chickpea Puree (page 147), is about the most comforting dinner you can possibly imagine.*

**5 pounds very meaty bone-in beef short ribs, cut into 2-inch chunks (see tip)**

**Good olive oil**

**Kosher salt and freshly ground black pepper**

**3 cups chopped leeks, white and light green parts (3 leeks)**

**3 cups chopped celery (5 to 6 ribs)**

**2 cups chopped yellow onions (2 onions)**

**2 cups chopped unpeeled carrots (6 carrots)**

**1½ tablespoons minced garlic (5 cloves)**

**1 (750-ml) bottle Burgundy, Côtes du Rhône, Chianti, or other dry red wine**

**4 cups beef stock, preferably homemade (page 260) or College Inn**

**1 cup canned crushed tomatoes, such as San Marzano**

**1 (11.2-ounce) bottle Guinness draught stout**

**6 sprigs fresh thyme, tied with kitchen string**

**Creamy Blue Cheese Grits (page 151) or Celery Root & Chickpea Puree (page 147), for serving**

**pro tip** Short ribs come in many sizes. Be sure you buy 2-inch ribs with lots of meat on them. Browning them on a sheet pan is so much easier—and less messy!—than in a pot on top of the stove.

**pro tip** Because garlic burns very easily, I almost never cook it with the onions; instead I add it one minute before adding the liquid.

Preheat the oven to 425 degrees. Place the short ribs on a sheet pan, brush the tops with olive oil, and sprinkle with 1½ tablespoons salt and 1½ teaspoons pepper. Roast for 20 minutes and remove from the oven. Reduce the temperature to 325 degrees.

Meanwhile, heat ¼ cup olive oil in a large (12-inch) Dutch oven, such as Le Creuset, over medium heat. Add the leeks, celery, onions, and carrots and cook over medium to medium-high heat for 20 minutes, stirring occasionally. Add the garlic and cook for one minute. Add the wine, bring to a boil, lower the heat, and simmer over medium heat for

*recipe continues*

10 minutes, until the liquid is reduced. Add the stock, tomatoes, Guinness, thyme, 1 tablespoon salt, and 1½ teaspoons pepper.

Place the ribs in the pot, along with the juices and seasonings from the sheet pan. Bring to a boil, cover, and cook in the oven for one hour. Uncover and cook for one more hour, until the meat is very tender.

Remove the short ribs to a plate with a slotted spoon and discard the thyme bundle and any bones that have separated from the meat. Simmer the sauce on the stove for 20 minutes, until reduced. Skim some of the fat off the top and discard. Return the ribs to the pot, heat for 5 minutes, and taste for seasonings. Serve hot in shallow bowls spooned over creamy blue cheese grits, with extra sauce on the side.

# roast duck breast
## with dried cherries & port

serves 4

*This is a very "pro" way to cook duck breast as it's often prepared in restaurants but it's easy to do at home. First, you salt the duck when you bring it home from the store to allow the seasoning to penetrate the meat. Next, sear the duck on top of the stove, then roast it in the oven, and finally, allow the meat to rest while you make the sauce with dried cherries and Port.*

**2 (1-pound) or 4 (8-ounce) Moulard duck breasts**
**Kosher salt and freshly ground black pepper**
**1 tablespoon canola oil**
**2 tablespoons unsalted butter**
**½ cup minced shallots (2 shallots)**
**1½ tablespoons good sherry wine vinegar**
**¾ cup ruby Port wine**
**½ cup good chicken stock, preferably homemade (page 259)**
**½ cup dried cherries**
**¼ cup crème fraîche**
**1 teaspoon grated orange zest**
**¼ cup freshly squeezed orange juice**

**pro tip** Test your instant-read thermometer by dipping it in a cup of boiling water; it should register 212 degrees. If not, it may need recalibrating by turning the bolt on the back slightly. Double-check by dipping it in a glass of ice water. If it doesn't register 32 degrees you may need to adjust a bit more.

Wrap each duck breast in plastic wrap and pound them with a meat mallet until each breast is about 1 inch thick. Place the duck on a plate, sprinkle both sides with a total of 4 teaspoons salt, cover with plastic wrap, and refrigerate for at least 6 hours or overnight.

When ready to cook the duck, preheat the oven to 375 degrees.

Score the skin of the duck breasts with a sharp knife, making a crosshatch pattern but not cutting down to the meat.

In a large (12-inch) heavy-bottomed, ovenproof skillet, heat the oil over medium heat. Place the duck breasts in the pan, skin side down. Cook uncovered over medium heat for 12 to 15 minutes, discarding the fat from the pan occasionally, until the skin is very browned. Turn the duck with tongs, place the skillet in the oven, and roast for 12 to 18 minutes, until the internal temperature of the duck is 120 degrees for rare. Remove from the oven, cover the pan tightly with aluminum foil, and allow the duck to rest for 10 minutes.

Meanwhile, make the sauce. Melt the butter over medium-high heat in a medium saucepan. Add the shallots and sauté for 2 minutes, until tender. Add the vinegar and cook for one minute. Add the Port, chicken stock, cherries, 1 teaspoon salt, and ½ teaspoon pepper, bring to a boil, lower the heat, and simmer for 15 minutes. Stir in the crème fraîche, orange zest, and orange juice and keep warm over low heat.

Transfer the duck to a cutting board and slice diagonally, fanning the slices out on 4 dinner plates. Spoon the sauce generously on top, sprinkle with salt, and serve hot with extra sauce on the side.

# roasted eggplant parmesan

serves 6

*Most recipes for eggplant Parmesan require that you fry the eggplant, which leaves my kitchen—and me!—a greasy mess. Instead, I roast the eggplant, and it's so much better. The rest is just layering the eggplant with lots of tomato sauce, basil, mozzarella, and a little tangy goat cheese. I particularly love the crunchy, garlicky bread crumbs on top.*

2½ pounds eggplant, unpeeled, halved lengthwise, and sliced
   ¼ to ⅓ inch thick (see tip, page 62)

¾ cup good olive oil

1 tablespoon dried oregano

Kosher salt and freshly ground black pepper

1 (24-ounce) jar marinara sauce, such as Rao's

½ cup julienned fresh basil leaves

1 pound fresh buffalo mozzarella, thinly sliced

8 ounces garlic and herb goat cheese, such as Montrachet

1½ cups freshly grated Italian Parmesan cheese

for the topping

1⅓ cups fresh bread crumbs from a country loaf

4 garlic cloves, minced

¼ cup chopped fresh basil or parsley leaves

¼ cup good olive oil

Preheat the oven to 400 degrees and arrange three racks evenly spaced.

Lay the eggplant in one layer on three sheet pans and brush both sides with olive oil, using all the oil. Sprinkle with the oregano, crushing it lightly in your hands, then sprinkle with 1½ tablespoons salt and 1½ teaspoons pepper. Bake for 15 minutes. Turn the slices and rotate the pans in the oven and bake for another 10 minutes, until tender. Leave the oven at 400 degrees.

In a 10 × 14 × 2-inch ceramic baking dish, spread a third of the marinara sauce. Arrange a third of the eggplant on top in one layer. Scatter a third of the basil, a third of the mozzarella, a third of the goat cheese, and a third of the Parmesan on top. Repeat twice, starting with

*recipe continues*

the marinara and ending with the Parmesan, making sure each layer is evenly distributed.

For the topping, place the bread crumbs, garlic, and basil in a food processor and pulse to combine. Add the ¼ cup olive oil and 1 teaspoon salt and pulse to moisten the crumbs. Sprinkle the mixture evenly over the dish.

Bake for 45 to 50 minutes, until bubbling and golden brown. Allow to sit at room temperature for 10 minutes before serving.

# shells with broccoli rabe & pancetta

serves 4 to 5

*My friend Deborah Berke doesn't have much time to cook; besides running her busy architecture practice, she is also the dean of the Yale School of Architecture. Her favorite really fast dinner is a pasta recipe from* Italian Easy: Recipes from the London River Cafe *with broccoli rabe and pancetta. Here is my take on that dish, with a dollop of fresh ricotta on top for good measure.*

**Kosher salt and freshly ground black pepper**
**1½ pounds broccoli rabe (1 to 2 bunches)**
**1 pound large pasta shells, such as Barilla**
**Good olive oil**
**½ pound pancetta, ¼-inch diced (see tip)**
**2 garlic cloves, minced**
**1 teaspoon crushed red pepper flakes**
**8 to 10 ounces fresh ricotta, store-bought or**
    **homemade (page 264)**
**Freshly grated Italian Parmesan cheese, for serving**

Bring a large (11 × 5½-inch) pot of water to a boil and add 1 tablespoon salt. Remove and discard the bottom third of the broccoli rabe and slice the rest crosswise in 2-inch pieces. When the water boils, cook the broccoli rabe for 2 to 3 minutes, until just tender. With a wire skimmer or tongs, lift the broccoli rabe (don't drain the pot!) into a large bowl and set aside. Bring the water back to a boil, add the shells, and cook al dente according to the directions on the package. Reserve 1 cup of the cooking liquid, drain the pasta, and set aside.

Meanwhile, heat 2 tablespoons olive oil in a large (12-inch) sauté pan, add the pancetta, and cook over medium heat for 8 minutes, stirring occasionally, until the pancetta is browned. Add the garlic and cook for one minute. Add the broccoli rabe and red pepper flakes and toss well. Add the cooked shells, 1 teaspoon salt, and 1 teaspoon black pepper and toss. Cook over medium heat for a few minutes, until all the ingredients are heated through, adding enough of the reserved cooking water so the pasta isn't dry. Serve hot in large shallow bowls with a large dollop of ricotta and drizzled with olive oil, and with grated Parmesan on the side.

**pro tip** The only way to truly make ¼-inch-diced pancetta is to buy one big chunk and cut it yourself. Delis often slice it much too thin.

# shrimp & grits

serves 4

*I have always admired Christopher Kimball, the former publisher of* Cook's Illustrated *magazine and founder of Milk Street cooking school, magazine, and cookbook. I love his scientific approach to cooking and his charming professorial sensibility. I've tried a few variations of shrimp and grits, but this version, which is a slight tweak from Christopher's, is my favorite. It's creamy grits with spicy shrimp and bacon. Who wouldn't love that?*

6 tablespoons (¾ stick) unsalted butter, divided
1 cup quick-cooking (5-minute) grits, such as Quaker
2¼ cups whole milk
Kosher salt and freshly ground black pepper
1½ pounds (20-count) shrimp, peeled and shells reserved (see tip)
1 tablespoon tomato paste
2 slices thick-cut bacon, cut in ½-inch pieces, such as Nodine's
1 teaspoon minced garlic
2 tablespoons all-purpose flour
1 tablespoon freshly squeezed lemon juice
½ teaspoon Sriracha or Tabasco
4 scallions, white and green parts, thinly sliced diagonally

For the grits, melt 1 tablespoon of the butter in a medium saucepan over medium heat. Add the grits and cook for 3 minutes, stirring often. Add the milk, 2 cups water, and 1 teaspoon salt and bring to a boil. Lower the heat, cover, and simmer for 25 minutes, whisking occasionally to be sure the grits don't get lumpy. Off the heat, stir in 2 tablespoons of the butter, 1 teaspoon salt, and ½ teaspoon pepper. Cover and set aside to keep warm.

Meanwhile, heat 1 tablespoon of the butter in a large (12-inch) sauté pan over medium heat. Add the shrimp shells and cook for 5 to 7 minutes, stirring occasionally, until the shells are lightly browned. Stir in the tomato paste and cook for 30 seconds. Add 2 cups water and bring to a boil. Lower the heat, cover, and simmer for 5 minutes. Strain the liquid into a bowl, then pour into a glass measuring cup. Discard the shells, and add enough water to make 1½ cups of stock. Set aside.

Wipe out the sauté pan with a paper towel, add the bacon, and cook over medium heat for 5 to 7 minutes, until crisp. Stir in the shrimp, garlic, 1 teaspoon salt, and ½ teaspoon pepper and cook for 2 minutes. Transfer to a plate and set aside. Melt 1 tablespoon of the butter in the pan, whisk in the flour, and cook for one minute. Whisk in the stock, bring to a boil, reduce the heat, and simmer for 5 minutes, until thickened. Return the shrimp mixture to the pan, cover, and cook over medium heat for 3 minutes, until the shrimp are cooked through. Off the heat, stir in the lemon juice, Sriracha, and the remaining tablespoon of butter.

Serve large puddles of grits in large shallow bowls, spoon the shrimp and sauce on top, sprinkle with scallions, salt, and pepper and serve hot.

**pro tip** Grocery stores and seafood shops refer to shrimp differently. Labels such as "large" and "extra large" can be arbitrary. Order shrimp by the count per pound, rather than the size.

# spiced lamb-stuffed eggplants

serves 4

*I love lamb with Greek flavors like garlic, oregano, cinnamon, red wine, and tomatoes. This recipe takes a little while to make, but you can assemble it in advance and bake it just before serving. Each serving is two halves of a baby eggplant stuffed with lamb and topped with ricotta and goat cheese. So satisfying!*

4 baby eggplants (6 to 7 inches long and 8 to 10 ounces each (see note)
Good olive oil
Kosher salt and freshly ground black pepper
1½ cups chopped yellow onion
4 teaspoons minced garlic (4 cloves)
1 pound lean ground lamb
1 tablespoon dried oregano
1 teaspoon ground cinnamon
½ cup dry red wine
1 (14.5-ounce) can diced tomatoes, such as San Marzano, undrained
1 cup marinara sauce, such as Rao's
⅓ cup minced fresh parsley
1½ cups fresh ricotta (12 ounces)
4 ounces fresh goat cheese, such as Montrachet
2 extra-large egg yolks
1½ tablespoons julienned fresh mint leaves, plus extra for serving

Baby eggplants are thinner and smaller than regular eggplants or Japanese eggplants.

Preheat the oven to 375 degrees.

Cut the eggplants in half lengthwise, including the stems. Using a sharp paring knife, scoop out some of the flesh, leaving a shell that is ⅓ inch thick and reserving the scooped-out eggplant. Place the eggplant shells snugly in a single layer in a large (10 × 14-inch) rectangular baking dish. Brush the eggplant all over with ¼ cup olive oil (use it all!) and sprinkle with 1½ teaspoons salt and ¾ teaspoon pepper. Pour ¼ cup water in the baking dish, cover tightly with aluminum foil, and bake for 30 minutes, until the shells are tender when pierced with a small knife. Remove from the oven, discard the foil, and leave the oven on.

*recipe continues*

**pro tip** If you sauté onions in a large pot that has a lot of bottom surface right on the heat, they will cook more quickly and caramelize better than if you put them in a small pot where all they will do is steam in the oil or butter.

Meanwhile, for the lamb filling, in a large (12-inch) skillet, heat 3 tablespoons olive oil over medium heat. Add the onion and sauté for 5 minutes, tossing occasionally, until tender. Cut the reserved scooped-out eggplant into ½-inch dice (you should have about 2 cups). Add the eggplant to the onion and cook for 5 minutes, adding more oil if it seems dry. Add the garlic and cook for 30 seconds, until fragrant. Add the ground lamb and cook, mashing lightly with a fork, for 5 to 7 minutes, until no longer pink. Add the oregano and cinnamon and cook for one minute. Add the wine, tomatoes, marinara, parsley, 2 teaspoons salt, and 1 teaspoon pepper. Bring to a boil, lower the heat, and simmer uncovered for 25 to 30 minutes, until the liquid evaporates. Spoon the filling into the eggplant halves in the baking dish. (You may have a little extra filling.)

In a medium bowl, mash the ricotta, goat cheese, egg yolks, mint, 1 teaspoon salt, and ½ teaspoon pepper with a fork. With a spoon, place large dollops of the ricotta mixture on the lamb filling and bake for 30 to 40 minutes, until the filling is hot and the topping is lightly browned. Serve warm, sprinkled with extra mint.

# warm lobster rolls

serves 6

*Everybody knows classic lobster rolls, which consist of cold lobster salad with mayo in a hot dog bun. While there's nothing wrong with that, when I discovered there was something called a Connecticut lobster roll, which is warm lobster sautéed in butter served on a grilled bun, there was no going back. Lots of fresh herbs and lemon juice make this really special.*

**Perfect Poached Lobster (page 263) or**
    **1 pound cooked lobster meat**
**5 tablespoons unsalted butter, divided**
**½ cup small-diced celery**
**Kosher salt and freshly ground black pepper**
**½ teaspoon minced fresh dill, plus extra for garnish**
**½ teaspoon minced fresh parsley**
**Juice of 1 lemon**
**6 top-sliced hot dog buns, such as Pepperidge Farm**

Cut the lobster meat in large (¾-inch) dice. Heat 3 tablespoons of the butter in a medium (10-inch) sauté pan over medium-high heat. Add the lobster, celery, 1 teaspoon salt, and ½ teaspoon pepper and cook, stirring occasionally, for 2 to 3 minutes, until just heated through. Off the heat, sprinkle the lobster with the dill, parsley, and half of the lemon juice. Stir well.

Meanwhile, heat the remaining 2 tablespoons of butter in a large (12-inch) sauté pan, until the butter sizzles. Place the rolls in the pan on their sides (you are toasting the outsides, not the insides) and cook over medium-high heat for 2 minutes on each side, until nicely browned.

Place the rolls, cut side up, on a platter. Divide the lobster mixture among the 6 rolls and sprinkle with extra dill, salt, and the remaining lemon juice. Serve hot while the rolls are crisp on the outside and the lobster filling is hot.

vegetables
& sides

# cut like a pro

Like a surgeon choosing the right instrument, a chef not only needs to have good equipment but also needs to keep the equipment in good working order. My dad was a surgeon and at home he kept a pair of surgical scissors locked in a drawer because, of course, when he wasn't looking, we would try to use them to cut up our crayons and construction paper and would dull the blades. Use your kitchen knives *only* for cutting food—no opening coffee cans or hacking into FedEx boxes! If you take good care of your knives, you'll find that prep work not only is easier, but is so much more satisfying.

Knives come in lots of different shapes and sizes and from manufacturers all over the world. Choose high-quality knives with a "full tang" (this means the blade runs the full length of the handle) and that feel balanced and comfortable in your hand. Some cookware stores provide stations where you can try out a knife you are considering buying, and it's worth taking the time to give an expensive knife a test run before you invest.

It's also important to know how to keep your knives sharp. The best utensil for regular use is a sharpening steel, a long cylindrical instrument with a handle that you run along your knife blade at a specific angle to keep the edge straight and sharp. For more serious honing I particularly like an electric sharpener called Chef's Choice Professional Sharpening Station. It has grinding surfaces that hone the blade a little more coarsely at first, and then more finely. You don't want to use it every day because it does wear down your blade; but it's fantastic for sharpening a very dull knife and the machine holds the blade at exactly the right angle.

Always wash and dry your knives immediately after each use, and never, ever put them in the dishwasher, which dulls the blade and can harm the handle. Make sure to store them in such a way that the blade (and your fingers!) are protected. Don't let them rattle around loose in a drawer; invest in a drawer insert with slots for the blades, or a magnetic strip that attaches to a wall and holds the blades flat.

Here are some of the cutting implements that I use most (for knives, the measurement refers to the size of the blade alone, not the whole knife). The first four make up a basic set and the rest are specialty things that I use a lot. Choose those you'll use the most, based on which foods you like to prepare. And know that if you take good care of your knives, they'll return the favor and take good care of you for decades.

3½ to 5-inch paring knife for tasks like peeling fruit and hulling strawberries

5 to 7-inch santoku or chef's knife for slicing, dicing, and mincing fruits and vegetables

8 to 10-inch carving knife for slicing meats

8-inch serrated knife for slicing bread

5-inch serrated knife for slicing tomatoes

Dental floss for slicing soft cheeses such as goat cheese

# baked spinach & zucchini

serves 6

*No one taught me more about cooking than my late dear friend Anna Pump, who wrote many wonderful cookbooks. I think of her often but always when I'm making a dish inspired by her, such as this easy spinach and zucchini gratin.*

4 tablespoons (½ stick) unsalted butter, melted, divided
Good olive oil
6 scallions, white and green parts, sliced ¼ inch across
1 pound small zucchini, sliced in ¼-inch-thick rounds (4 zucchini)
1 tablespoon minced garlic (3 cloves)
2 (10-ounce) packages frozen chopped spinach, defrosted
1 cup cooked basmati rice
¼ cup chopped fresh basil leaves
¼ cup chopped fresh parsley
½ teaspoon ground nutmeg
2 tablespoons freshly squeezed lemon juice
Kosher salt and freshly ground black pepper
4 extra-large eggs
¾ cup heavy cream
¼ cup freshly grated Italian Parmesan cheese, plus extra
2 ounces Gruyère cheese, grated

**pro tip** It looks very professional to bake this in individual cast-iron pans.

Preheat the oven to 350 degrees. Grease a 9 × 14 × 2-inch oval baking dish with 2 tablespoons of the melted butter and set aside.

Heat 2 tablespoons olive oil in a large (12-inch) sauté pan over medium-high heat. Add the scallions and zucchini and sauté for 2 minutes. Add the garlic and cook for one minute. Lightly press most of the water out of the spinach and add it to the pan. Add the rice, basil, parsley, nutmeg, lemon juice, 2 teaspoons salt, and 1 teaspoon pepper and toss well. Transfer to the prepared baking dish.

In a medium bowl, whisk together the eggs, cream, the remaining 2 tablespoons melted butter, and the ¼ cup Parmesan. Pour the mixture over the spinach and zucchini and smooth the top. Sprinkle with some extra Parmesan and the Gruyère. Bake for 20 to 30 minutes, until a knife inserted in the center comes out clean.

**pro tip** To be sure you are getting true aged Parmesan from Italy, grate your own cheese by grinding it in a food processor. Pre-grated cheeses, even from a specialty food store, are often made from lesser quality Parmesan.

# celery root & chickpea puree

serves 6

*In the winter when I make any kind of roasted meat, I like to serve something creamy and comforting with it. There's nothing wrong with great mashed potatoes, but I'm always looking for an alternative. This puree has a texture similar to coarsely mashed potatoes, but has lots of flavor from the celery root, chickpeas, lemon, and Parmesan cheese.*

**6 cups peeled, ¾-inch-diced celery root (2½ pounds)**

**2 cups good chicken stock, preferably homemade (page 259)**

**1 (1 pound 13-ounce) can chickpeas, rinsed and drained**

**Good olive oil**

**1 teaspoon minced fresh thyme leaves**

**½ teaspoon grated lemon zest**

**1 tablespoon freshly squeezed lemon juice**

**Kosher salt and freshly ground black pepper**

**¼ cup freshly grated Italian Parmesan cheese,**
   **plus extra for serving**

Place the celery root and chicken stock in a large saucepan and bring to a boil. Lower the heat, cover, and simmer for 15 to 20 minutes, until the celery root is very tender. Add the drained chickpeas, return to a simmer, and cook for 3 minutes, until heated through.

Carefully pour the celery root and chickpea mixture, including the liquid, into the bowl of a food processor fitted with the steel blade, and process until coarsely pureed. (You may need to do this in batches.) Return the puree to the saucepan and reheat over low heat.

In a 1-cup glass measuring cup, combine ¼ cup olive oil, the thyme, lemon zest, lemon juice, 1 tablespoon salt, and 1 teaspoon pepper, and whisk it into the puree. Off the heat, stir in the Parmesan. Taste for seasonings and serve hot with an extra sprinkling of Parmesan.

**pro tip** Remove thyme leaves from the sprigs by running your fingers backward over the stem.

**make ahead:** Prepare the puree completely except for the Parmesan cheese. Reheat with a little extra chicken stock or water over medium-low heat. Off the heat, stir in the Parmesan before serving.

# chipotle parmesan sweet corn

serves 6 to 8

*When the corn is in season in East Hampton, I just can't make enough of it. One of my great pleasures is going to Pike Farms in Sagaponack, New York, and buying their delicious corn. This recipe is the essence of simplicity so be sure the corn is sweet and tender. Be careful with the chipotle powder; too much can overpower the flavor of the corn! You want the perfect balance of sweet corn and salty Parmesan, with a little chipotle heat.*

6 tablespoons (¾ stick) unsalted butter

1 cup shallots, halved lengthwise, peeled, and thinly sliced crosswise (3 shallots)

8 cups white or yellow corn kernels (8 to 12 ears) (see tip)

¼ teaspoon chipotle chile powder

Kosher salt and freshly ground black pepper

2 tablespoons freshly squeezed lime juice

1 tablespoon freshly grated Italian Parmesan cheese

Heat the butter in a large (12-inch) sauté pan over medium heat, add the shallots, and cook for about 5 minutes, until tender and fragrant. Add the corn, chipotle powder, 2 teaspoons salt, and 1 teaspoon pepper. Raise the heat to medium high and cook for 10 to 12 minutes, stirring occasionally to allow the corn to brown lightly, until the corn is tender but still firm. Off the heat, stir in the lime juice and Parmesan. Taste for seasonings and transfer to a large shallow serving bowl. Serve hot.

**pro tip** Shuck the corn, then brush it with a clean vegetable brush to remove the remaining silk. Place a clean kitchen towel on a sheet pan. Cut the stem end of the cob straight across, stand the cob upright on its end, and cut the kernels onto the towel so the kernels don't bounce all over the kitchen. Pick up the towel and pour the kernels into the pan.

# creamy blue cheese grits

serves 6

*Grits, or hominy grits, are made from dried corn from which the hull and germ have been removed. The box may say the grits cook in five minutes, but for this recipe I cook them for a full fifty minutes, until they're smooth and creamy. Of course, adding half-and-half, butter, and Roquefort cheese will make anything taste better!*

**Kosher salt and freshly ground black pepper**
**1½ cups quick-cooking (5-minute) grits, such as Quaker**
**2 cups half-and-half**
**3 tablespoons unsalted butter**
**3 ounces Roquefort, crumbled**

Bring 6 cups water to a full rolling boil in a heavy 4-quart saucepan. Add 1 tablespoon salt and slowly whisk in the grits, pouring them into the pot in a thin, steady stream while whisking constantly. Reduce the heat to low and simmer, stirring occasionally, for 5 to 7 minutes, until the grits have thickened.

Add the half-and-half and butter and stir. It will seem very thin but the grits will thicken again as they cook. Bring the grits to a boil over medium heat, reduce the heat, cover, and simmer for 45 minutes, stirring occasionally, until smooth and creamy. Off the heat, stir in the Roquefort, 1 teaspoon salt, and 1 teaspoon pepper. Season to taste and serve hot.

**make ahead:** You can make this early in the day, refrigerate it, and reheat with a little extra water. If you refrigerate the grits for more than 24 hours, however, they will separate and never come together again.

# haricots verts with hazelnuts & dill

serves 6

*The French chef Joël Robuchon has been known to say he limits his dishes to no more than three dominant flavors so you appreciate the intrinsic flavors of a dish. Of course, I'm sure he didn't mean that literally, because some subtle flavorings simply make other ingredients taste better, but I like his philosophy. Here I flavor French string beans with toasted hazelnuts and fresh dill, and I think they all work really well together.*

½ cup whole hazelnuts (see tip)
Kosher salt and freshly ground black pepper
1½ pounds French string beans (haricots verts),
    stem ends removed
1 tablespoon unsalted butter
Good olive oil
¼ cup minced fresh dill

**pro tip** When cooking with any kind of nuts, I often toast them before adding them to a recipe because it brings out their flavor and crisps them.

Place the hazelnuts in a large (12-inch) sauté pan set over medium heat. Cook for 5 to 10 minutes, rolling them around occasionally, until they are heated through. Transfer the nuts to a clean kitchen towel, fold the towel over, and roll them around until some of the skins fall off. (Don't worry if they don't all fall off.) Roughly chop the hazelnuts and set aside. Wipe out the pan with a kitchen towel.

Meanwhile, fill a large pot with 4 quarts water, add 1 tablespoon salt, and bring to a boil. Plunge the string beans into the water and cook for 5 minutes, until just tender. Drain immediately, plunge into a large bowl of ice water, and set aside.

When ready to serve, heat the butter and 1 tablespoon olive oil in the large sauté pan over medium-high heat. Add the string beans, 2 teaspoons salt, and 1 teaspoon pepper and cook for 3 minutes, stirring with tongs, until heated through. Off the heat, stir in the dill and hazelnuts and taste for seasonings. Serve hot.

# maple-roasted acorn squash

serves 6

*When I was growing up, my mother served a lot of canned vegetables, but the one thing she always made from scratch was acorn squash, which she roasted with butter and maple syrup. When I revisited her old method, I found it was just as good as I remembered. The sweet squash filled with a big puddle of melted butter and sweet syrup is so irresistible!*

**3 acorn squash, unpeeled, halved through the stem, and seeded**
**3 tablespoons unsalted butter, diced**
**3 tablespoons pure maple syrup, plus extra for serving**
**Good olive oil**
**Kosher salt and freshly ground black pepper**
**Flaked sea salt, such as Maldon, for serving**

Preheat the oven to 350 degrees.

Place the squash, cut sides up, on a sheet pan. Place ½ tablespoon butter and ½ tablespoon maple syrup in the cavity of each squash. Brush the cut sides with olive oil and sprinkle the squash with 3 teaspoons kosher salt and 1 teaspoon pepper. Roast for 40 to 60 minutes, depending on the size of the squash, until tender when pierced with a small knife.

Place the squash on a serving platter. If the halves are too large for one serving, cut each piece in half through the stem. Drizzle lightly with extra maple syrup, sprinkle with sea salt, and serve hot.

**pro tip** Acorn squash is hard to cut. To halve a whole squash, plunge the blade of a large chef's knife into the side of the squash as far as it will go. Holding the handle of the knife, bang the squash (with the knife in it) on the board until the blade cuts all the way through.

# orange-roasted rainbow carrots

serves 4

*It used to be that carrots came in only one color: orange. Now you can get carrots in all sorts of colors, and while they pretty much all taste the same, using a mix of colors makes any carrot dish so much more appealing. Roasting carrots at a high temperature sweetens them by caramelizing their sugars; and finishing them with orange zest, orange juice, and sea salt gives them so much flavor.*

**1 pound orange carrots, unpeeled**
**1 pound rainbow carrots, unpeeled**
**Good olive oil**
**Kosher salt and freshly ground black pepper**
**1 teaspoon grated orange zest (see tip)**
**2 tablespoons freshly squeezed orange juice**
**1 teaspoon fleur de sel**

Preheat the oven to 450 degrees.

Remove the tops and scrub the orange and rainbow carrots with a vegetable brush. Cut the carrots in long diagonal slices. (You want fairly uniform sticks about 4 inches long by ½ inch wide.)

Place the carrots on a sheet pan, drizzle with 3 tablespoons olive oil, and sprinkle with 1 teaspoon kosher salt and ½ teaspoon pepper. Toss well with your hands and spread out in one layer.

Roast for 15 to 20 minutes, turning once, until the carrots are lightly browned and tender. Sprinkle with the orange zest, orange juice, and fleur de sel and toss well. Serve hot or at room temperature.

**pro tip** When I use citrus juice in a recipe, I often add the zest as well for even more flavor.

# parmesan pesto zucchini sticks

serves 6 to 8

*We test and retest my recipes to make sure anyone can make them, and I'm always quizzing my assistants Barbara and Lidey to find out what they think of the finished dish. After retesting this zucchini, Barbara exclaimed, "I'm making these again tonight!"—which is basically the highest compliment. The pesto and garlic make the zucchini taste amazing.*

3 medium (6 to 8-inch-long) zucchini, trimmed

½ cup good store-bought pesto

8 tablespoons good olive oil, divided

¼ cup roughly chopped fresh flat-leaf parsley

2 large garlic cloves

1¼ cups panko (Japanese bread flakes)

¾ cup freshly grated Italian Parmesan cheese

Pinch of crushed red pepper flakes

Kosher salt and freshly ground black pepper

Flaked sea salt, such as Maldon, for sprinkling

Preheat the oven to 400 degrees. Arrange two racks evenly spaced in the oven. Line two sheet pans with parchment paper.

Cut each zucchini in quarters lengthwise through the stem and then cut each quarter again in thirds lengthwise, making long skinny spears. In a medium shallow bowl, whisk together the pesto and 4 tablespoons of the olive oil and set aside. Place the parsley and garlic in the bowl of a food processor fitted with the steel blade and process until they are finely minced. Add the panko, Parmesan, red pepper flakes, 1 teaspoon kosher salt, and ½ teaspoon black pepper plus the remaining 4 table-spoons olive oil. Pulse only until all the panko is moistened with oil. Pour the mixture onto a dinner plate.

Dip the zucchini spears first into the pesto mixture, turning to coat completely, then place each one in the crumb mixture, pressing and turning to coat thickly. Arrange the sticks in rows on the prepared sheet pans.

Roast for 20 to 30 minutes, until the zucchini is tender and the crumbs have crisped to a crunchy golden brown. Sprinkle lightly with flaked sea salt and serve hot.

**pro tip** To mince fresh green herbs like dill, parsley, and cilantro, first run the sharp edge of your knife up the stems to remove the fronds or leaves. Discard the stems, and then mince the herbs.

# perfect basmati rice

serves 6 to 8

*I love basmati rice when it's made right, but if you simply follow the directions on the package, it often turns out gummy and bland. My friend Sarah Chase showed me that with a little more effort, you end up with divine, fluffy, and fla- vorful basmati rice. Trust me; once you've tried this method, you won't go back.*

**2 cups basmati rice, such as Texmati Long Grain American
    Basmati rice**
**¼ cup canola oil**
**2 teaspoons kosher salt**
**3 cups boiling water**
**2 tablespoons unsalted butter, diced**

Rest a sieve in a bowl. Pour the rice in the sieve and fill the bowl with cold water, immersing the rice. Lift the sieve, discard the water, and repeat several times, until the water in the bowl is clear. Place the sieve with the rice back in the bowl, fill the bowl with water, and allow the rice to soak for 20 minutes. Drain well.

Heat the oil in a medium (8 × 4-inch) saucepan over medium heat. Stir in the rice and salt and cook for one minute, until the rice is hot and the grains are covered with oil. Stir in the boiling water, raise the heat until it comes to a full rolling boil, lower the heat, cover tightly, and simmer for 10 minutes exactly (you may need to pull the pot slightly off the heat to keep it at a simmer). Keep the lid on—don't even peek! Turn off the heat and allow the rice to sit with the lid on for 10 more minutes. Add the butter, fluff the rice with a fork, and serve hot.

# potato galette

serves 4

A mandoline makes short work of slicing long matchsticks.

**pro tip** Combining oil and butter gets the best of both ingredients—the high burning temperature of oil for a golden and crispy crust and the delicious flavor of butter.

**make ahead:** Prepare up to an hour ahead and reheat the galette in a 400-degree oven for 5 minutes.

*My assistant Lidey Heuck took a course at the International Culinary Center in New York City, and she came back with this very delicious, very simple recipe for a classic potato galette. I love the crispy outside and the flavorful, creamy inside. It's great with lamb or chicken, and I even serve it with scrambled eggs for breakfast, instead of hash browns.*

> 1¼ pounds russet baking potatoes (2 large)
> Kosher salt and freshly ground black pepper
> Canola oil
> 1½ tablespoons unsalted butter, at room temperature
> Minced chives, for serving
> Fleur de sel, for serving

Peel the potatoes and drop them in a bowl of cold water to keep them from turning brown. Using the small julienne blade of a mandoline, cut the potatoes lengthwise in long matchsticks. Place the potatoes on a clean kitchen towel and squeeze the towel to dry the potatoes without breaking them up. Place the potatoes in a bowl and toss them with 1 teaspoon salt and ½ teaspoon pepper.

Heat 2 tablespoons oil in a small (8-inch) sauté pan with sloped sides over medium heat. Add all the potatoes to the pan and arrange them so they lie flat (the pan will be very full!). Press them lightly with a metal spatula. Allow the potatoes to cook undisturbed for 5 minutes. Drizzle 1 tablespoon oil down the sides of the pan around the galette and cook for another 5 minutes. When the galette is nicely browned on the bottom, loosen it carefully around the edge with a large, narrow, flexible metal spatula and flip it over with a large flat spatula. (Be careful! The oil in the pan is very hot!) Cook the galette for 2 minutes. With the tip of a knife, run the pat of butter around the edges of the galette, allowing it to melt down the sides. Continue to cook for 4 to 5 minutes, until nicely browned on the second side. With the large flat spatula, transfer the galette to a paper towel and allow it to sit for 30 seconds. Transfer to a board and cut in quarters with a large chef's knife. Transfer to a plate, sprinkle with chives and fleur de sel, and serve hot.

# roasted broccoli with panko gremolata

serves 6

*Once I started roasting vegetables, I never wanted to go back to boiling or steaming them, because roasting brings out so much more flavor. The key to this recipe is spreading the broccoli out on two sheet pans, so the edges get nicely browned. Tossing it with toasted panko, garlic, lemon zest, and pine nuts makes this a crowd-pleasing party dish.*

2 large bunches broccoli

Good olive oil

Kosher salt and freshly ground black pepper

2 teaspoons minced garlic (2 cloves)

½ cup panko (Japanese bread flakes)

2 teaspoons grated lemon zest (2 lemons)

2 tablespoons toasted pine nuts (see tip)

1½ tablespoons freshly squeezed lemon juice

Preheat the oven to 400 degrees and arrange two racks evenly spaced.

Remove and discard the bottom half of the broccoli stems. Cut the remaining stems in half lengthwise up to the florets and pull (don't slice) the florets apart. Continue cutting all the stems lengthwise and pulling the florets apart; you want to have about 2 inches of stem with whole florets attached. Place the broccoli in a large bowl, drizzle with 4 tablespoons olive oil, sprinkle with 1½ teaspoons salt and 1 teaspoon pepper, and toss well. Divide the broccoli between two sheet pans, spreading the florets in one layer, and roast for 15 minutes, until crisp-tender and the edges are starting to brown, tossing occasionally.

Meanwhile, in a small (8-inch) sauté pan over medium-low heat, heat 1½ tablespoons olive oil, add the garlic, and cook for one minute, until fragrant but not browned. Add the panko, tossing to coat in the oil. Cook over medium-low heat for 3 to 4 minutes, until the panko is golden brown, tossing occasionally. Off the heat, add the lemon zest, pine nuts, lemon juice, the panko mixture, and ½ teaspoon salt. Toss well and serve hot, warm, or at room temperature.

**pro tip** Toast pine nuts in a small sauté pan over very low heat, tossing often until lightly browned. Pay attention; they burn quickly!

# butternut squash gratin

serves 6

*I know I use butternut squash in many of my recipes, but I love it. In the fall, this is an easy dish to dress up a simple roast chicken or pork loin. I cook the squash with garlic and a little nutmeg, then put it in a gratin dish with a topping of crunchy bread crumbs and Gruyère cheese. This is serious comfort food on a cold winter night.*

3 tablespoons unsalted butter, divided

Good olive oil

3 cups halved and thinly sliced yellow onions (2 large)

1 tablespoon minced garlic (3 cloves)

2 pounds butternut squash, peeled, halved, seeded, and sliced crosswise ⅛ inch thick

½ teaspoon ground nutmeg

Kosher salt and freshly ground black pepper

½ cup heavy cream

2 cups coarse fresh bread crumbs from a country loaf

½ cup grated Gruyère cheese (2 ounces)

Preheat the oven to 350 degrees. Use 1 tablespoon of the butter to grease an 8½ × 11½-inch oval baking dish.

In a large (12-inch) pot or Dutch oven, such as Le Creuset, heat the remaining 2 tablespoons of butter and 1 tablespoon olive oil over medium heat. Add the onions and garlic and cook, stirring occasionally, for 6 to 8 minutes, until tender. Stir in the squash, nutmeg, 2 teaspoons salt, and ¾ teaspoon pepper, cover, and cook for 10 minutes, stirring occasionally.

Spoon the squash mixture into the prepared baking dish and smooth the top, making sure all of the squash slices are laid flat. Pour the cream over the mixture. In a medium bowl, combine the bread crumbs and 2 tablespoons olive oil and mix in the Gruyère. Sprinkle evenly over the squash. Bake for 35 to 40 minutes, until the top is browned and the squash is very tender when tested in the center with a small knife. Sprinkle with salt and serve hot.

# sautéed savoy cabbage with bacon

serves 6

*Savoy cabbage is that wrinkled variety you've seen in the grocery store but never knew what to do with. It's more tender than traditional cabbage and I love its milder flavor. In the winter, when I serve roast pork, this is the perfect side dish. I sauté the cabbage with some butter and smoky bacon plus lots of salt and pepper—it's simple and delicious!*

8 ounces thick-cut applewood-smoked bacon, such as Nodine's
4 tablespoons (½ stick) unsalted butter
1 Savoy cabbage, including green outer leaves (2½ pounds)
Kosher salt and freshly ground black pepper

Cut the bacon crosswise in ¾-inch pieces. Heat a large (12-inch) sauté pan, add the bacon, and cook over medium heat for 10 minutes, stirring occasionally, until the bacon is browned and crisp. Transfer with a slotted spoon to a small dish lined with paper towels and set aside. Pour off all but ¼ cup of the bacon fat and discard. Add the butter to the pan and allow it to melt.

Meanwhile, shred the cabbage: cut the head in half through the core, remove the core, and slice the cabbage very thinly, making long shreds the way you would cut coleslaw. Add the cabbage to the pan with 1 tablespoon salt and 1½ teaspoons pepper and toss well. (It will seem like a lot in the pan but it will cook down.) Cook over medium heat for 5 minutes, tossing often, until the cabbage begins to soften. Raise the heat to medium high and cook for another 5 to 8 minutes, until the cabbage is tender and starting to brown. Add the bacon, toss well, taste for seasonings, and serve hot.

# warm brown rice
## & butternut squash

serves 6 to 8

*I like many kinds of rices, but I particularly like Texmati long-grain brown bas-mati rice. The nutty flavor is delicious with the sweet roasted butternut squash, tart dried cranberries, salty Marcona almonds, and orange and balsamic vinaigrette.*

**4 cups (½ to ¾-inch-diced) butternut squash (1½ pounds)**

**2 tablespoons plus ½ cup good olive oil, divided**

**2 tablespoons pure maple syrup, divided**

**Kosher salt and freshly ground black pepper**

**1½ cups brown rice, such as Texmati long-grain basmati**

**3 tablespoons freshly squeezed orange juice**

**1 tablespoon balsamic vinegar**

**1 tablespoon good white wine vinegar**

**2 teaspoons Dijon mustard, such as Grey Poupon**

**4 scallions, thinly cut diagonally, white and green parts**

**⅔ cup dried cranberries**

**½ cup salted Marcona almonds**

**pro tip** Marcona almonds are Spanish almonds that are roasted with olive oil and seasoned with sea salt. They can be a little harder to find than regular almonds, but they have so much more flavor that they're worth the effort.

Preheat the oven to 400 degrees.

Place the butternut squash on a sheet pan. Add 2 tablespoons of the olive oil, 1 tablespoon of the maple syrup, 2 teaspoons salt, and 1 tea-spoon pepper. Toss together, spread out in a single layer, and roast for 30 minutes, tossing twice, until tender and starting to brown.

Meanwhile, in a large saucepan, combine the rice, 3¼ cups water, and 1½ teaspoons salt. Bring to a boil, stir, lower the heat, cover, and simmer for 25 minutes. Turn off the heat and allow the rice to sit with the lid on for 10 minutes. (This will differ from the directions on the package.) If there is liquid left in the pot, drain the rice.

For the vinaigrette, in a glass measuring cup, whisk together the remaining 1 tablespoon of maple syrup, the orange juice, balsamic vinegar, white wine vinegar, mustard, 2 teaspoons salt, and 1 teaspoon pepper. Slowly whisk in ½ cup olive oil and set aside.

Pour the warm rice into a large serving bowl. Add most of the vinaigrette and combine. Add the squash, scallions, dried cranberries, and almonds and toss well. (As the dish sits, it may need the extra vinaigrette.) Taste for seasonings and serve warm or at room temperature.

dessert

campari & orange granita  178

chocolate chevron cake  180

chocolate pecan meringue torte  183

summer fruit tart  187

salted caramel sundae  191

fresh berries & sweet ricotta  195

rum raisin apple strudel with rum glaze  197

fresh fig & ricotta cake  201

moscato poached fruit  205

fresh peach cremolata  206

raspberry baked alaska  209

Leave the butter and eggs on the counter overnight so they come to room temperature.

If you forget to bring eggs to room temperature, place the uncracked eggs in a large bowl of warm water for five to ten minutes.

Use an ice cream scoop to measure out cookies and muffins in consistent sizes to ensure they bake evenly.

Practice makes perfect when learning how to handle a pastry bag.

Prep your ingredients in advance and check to be sure you've included every one.

Lining baking pans with parchment is the best way to ensure cakes release easily.

# bake like a pro

Lots of people tell me they can't bake. Cook, yes, but their baking always comes out wrong. The truth is, cooking requires less precision because you can adjust the recipe along the way. If it's too bland, you can add some salt. Sauce is too thin? Add a little butter and flour to thicken it. But baking is really different. Once you've prepared the batter, poured it into a pan, and it goes into the oven, you have no idea how it will taste until it's done cooking.

If you've made a few cakes that came out dry and cracked or didn't have lovely rounded tops, you may have decided that you simply just can't bake. It's not true. Once you know a few important things, trust me, your baking will be great.

Baking is very scientific. Follow the recipe exactly—this isn't the time to decide that mashed bananas would be good in the Fresh Fig & Ricotta Cake (page 201) if you have no idea what the extra fruit and moisture will do to the batter. Each ingredient needs to be measured precisely (see page 44 for more on that) and needs to be at the right temperature. In order for the butter to mix with sugar and become light and fluffy, as for a cake batter, it needs to be at room temperature. It won't get soft enough if you leave it on the counter for an hour; it takes hours for it to go from refrigerated temperature (38 degrees) to room temperature (70 degrees). Other recipes like Chocolate Pecan Scones (page 252) call for *cold* butter, which creates light and flaky pastry. Always read the recipe ahead of time to see which you'll need.

Plan a little extra time to preheat your oven. You can't set the oven to 350 degrees and think it will reach the right temperature in five minutes. An oven repairman once explained to me that when an oven heats up, it goes way above the set temperature, then falls back below the set temperature for about twenty minutes before it settles into a temperature that is dependable for baking. And always arrange the oven racks so whatever you're baking sits squarely in the center of the oven. You'll be surprised what a difference in temperature there can be between the top, bottom, and sides of your oven. Observe these simple guidelines and you, too, will be baking like a pro!

# campari & orange granita

serves 6

*Granita is perfect after a big dinner, because it's a light and refreshing dessert that's so easy to make. Campari and orange juice is one of my favorite drinks, so I thought, Why not make it into a granita? It's a little sweet and a little bitter— and definitely just for grown-ups!*

**1 cup sugar**
**3 cups freshly squeezed orange juice (6 to 8 oranges)**
**1 cup Campari**
**¼ cup freshly squeezed lemon juice**

**pro tip** If the granita freezes too hard, you can always defrost and refreeze it again.

For the sugar syrup, combine the sugar and 1 cup water in a small saucepan, bring to a boil, and cook just until the sugar is dissolved.

Pour the sugar syrup into a 10 × 13 × 2-inch ceramic (non-metal) dish and stir in the orange juice, Campari, and lemon juice. Place the dish on a level surface in the freezer and freeze for one hour. Rake the entire mixture, including the edges, with the tines of a dinner fork and freeze for another 30 minutes. Continue raking and freezing the granita every 30 minutes, until it's firm and granular. It should take 2 to 3 hours total. The granita is best served within a few hours. Spoon the granita into pretty bowls or stemmed martini glasses and serve frozen.

# chocolate chevron cake

makes one 8-inch cake

*This is a rich, dense chocolate cake that I've been making for decades. While the chevron design might look complicated, it's actually pretty easy and it makes a simple cake look incredibly professional. Even you won't believe you made it yourself!*

8 tablespoons (1 stick) unsalted butter, at room temperature

1 cup sugar

4 extra-large eggs, at room temperature

1 (16-ounce) can Hershey's chocolate syrup (1⅓ cups)

1 tablespoon pure vanilla extract

1 cup all-purpose flour

1 cup confectioners' sugar

## for the ganache

½ cup heavy cream

8 ounces semisweet chocolate chips, such as Hershey's

1 teaspoon instant coffee granules

**pro tip** You can wrap and refrigerate the cake for a few days, but once it is ganached, leave it at room temperature for up to 8 hours. If you refrigerate it, beads of condensation will form on the ganache and damage the decoration.

Preheat the oven to 325 degrees. Butter an 8 × 2-inch round cake pan, line the bottom with parchment paper, then butter and flour the pan, tapping out the excess flour.

Cream the butter and sugar in the bowl of an electric mixer fitted with the paddle attachment until light and fluffy. With the mixer on low, add the eggs, one at a time, then mix in the chocolate syrup and vanilla. Add the flour and mix until just combined. Pour the batter into the prepared pan and bake for 40 to 45 minutes, until just set in the middle. Allow to cool in the pan for 30 minutes, then remove from the pan, turn the cake upside down on a wire rack set over a sheet pan, and cool completely.

For the icing, whisk together the confectioners' sugar with 1 table-spoon water until smooth, thick, and just barely pourable. When you lift the icing from the bowl with the whisk, it should slowly fall back on itself in a ribbon. (You may need to add a few more drops of water.) Fit a pastry bag with a small, round pastry tip and fill it with the icing. Set aside while you make the ganache.

For the ganache, place the heavy cream, chocolate chips, and coffee in a bowl set over a pan of simmering water and heat the mixture until smooth and warm, stirring occasionally. Pour the ganache evenly over the top and sides of the cake, tilting the rack until the ganache is smooth all over.

Immediately, before the ganache sets, pipe parallel lines about 1 inch apart on the entire cake, stopping just short of the edge. Lightly drag the back of a small paring knife through the ganache perpendicular to the white lines also 1 inch apart, alternating directions (first left to right, then right to left, and so on) and covering the whole cake. Allow the ganache and icing to set. Cut in wedges and serve at room temperature.

# chocolate pecan meringue torte

serves 8

*When my late friend Anna Pump came to the United States from Germany, she started a cooking school in New Jersey, where she lived. This is one of the recipes she taught her students. It's two disks of crisp and soft meringue, layered with a creamy chocolate pecan filling. Your guests will be very impressed that you served such a professional-looking dessert!*

**7 extra-large egg whites, at room temperature**
**½ teaspoon cream of tartar**
**½ teaspoon kosher salt**
**2⅓ cups plus 2 tablespoons sugar, divided**
**2 teaspoons pure vanilla extract, divided**
**Chocolate Pecan Filling (recipe follows)**
**1 cup cold heavy cream**
**Dark chocolate shavings, for decorating (see tip)**

Preheat the oven to 250 degrees. Draw two 8-inch circles on a sheet of parchment paper and place it on a sheet pan, pencil side down.

In the bowl of an electric mixer fitted with the whisk attachment, beat the egg whites, cream of tartar, and salt on high speed for one minute, until frothy. With the mixer on high, slowly add the 2⅓ cups sugar and 1 teaspoon of the vanilla and beat on high for 2 minutes, until it makes firm, glossy peaks.

Divide the meringue between the two circles and spread into two flat 8-inch disks with a rubber spatula. Bake the meringues for one hour, turn the heat off, and leave the meringues in the oven for 2 hours. Remove them from the oven and allow to cool completely to room temperature on the sheet pan.

With a large flat spatula, carefully transfer one disk, rounded side up, to a totally flat serving plate. (It's okay if the top cracks a little.) Spread the chocolate pecan filling evenly on top. Place the second meringue, rounded side up, on top.

Combine the heavy cream, the 2 tablespoons sugar, and the remaining 1 teaspoon of vanilla in the bowl of an electric mixer fitted with the whisk attachment and beat on high speed until it forms firm peaks. Spread the whipped cream on top of the torte. Decorate with the shaved chocolate and refrigerate for 2 hours or for up to a day and serve cold.

**pro tip** To make chocolate curls, place a bar of chocolate in the microwave for 15 seconds before shaving it with a vegetable peeler.

# chocolate pecan filling

filling for one torte

½ cup pecans

4 extra-large eggs

¼ cup sugar

½ teaspoon cornstarch

4 ounces bittersweet chocolate, such as Lindt, broken in pieces

2 tablespoons brewed espresso

1 teaspoon Kahlúa

1 teaspoon pure vanilla extract

8 tablespoons (1 stick) unsalted butter, at room temperature (see tip)

**pro tip** Be sure the butter is completely at room temperature or the filling will be lumpy.

In the bowl of a food processor fitted with the steel blade, process the pecans until finely ground. Set aside.

In a medium bowl set over a pan of simmering water, whisk the eggs, sugar, and cornstarch together, making sure the bottom of the bowl doesn't touch the water. Whisk the mixture almost constantly, until it is 130 to 140 degrees and thickened like custard. Set aside to cool to room temperature, whisking occasionally.

Set another bowl over the pan of simmering water, making sure the bottom of the bowl doesn't touch the water. Put the chocolate and espresso in the bowl and heat just until the chocolate melts, stirring occasionally. Stir in the Kahlúa and vanilla and set aside to cool to room temperature. Whisk the chocolate mixture into the egg mixture, then whisk in the butter, one tablespoon at a time, whisking until smooth. Stir in the pecans. The filling can sit at room temperature for up to 4 hours.

# summer fruit tart

serves 8

*My favorite dessert has always been the simplest—the French Apple Tart in my book* Back to Basics. *It's a thin, crisp pastry crust with sliced apples, butter, and sugar on top. I was at my local farm stand and wondered, Why can't I make the same tart with other fruit? I tried it with peaches, figs, and plums all on one tart to see which I liked best, and I decided I liked all three together: juicy peaches, sweet figs, and tart plums.*

### for the pastry
**2 cups all-purpose flour**
**1 tablespoon sugar**
**½ teaspoon kosher salt**
**12 tablespoons (1½ sticks) cold unsalted butter, diced**
**½ cup ice water**

### for the fruit
**3 to 4 ripe peaches**
**6 large fresh figs**
**2 ripe plums**
**½ cup sugar**
**4 tablespoons (½ stick) cold unsalted butter, small-diced**
**½ cup apricot jelly (or apricot jam, heated and sieved)**

For the pastry, place the flour, sugar, and salt in the bowl of a food processor fitted with the steel blade. Pulse a few times to combine. Add the butter and pulse 10 to 12 times, until the butter is the size of peas. With the motor running, pour the ice water down the feed tube and pulse *just* until the dough starts to come together. Dump onto a floured board and knead quickly into a 5-inch-round flat disk. Wrap in plastic and refrigerate for exactly one hour (see tip).

Preheat the oven to 400 degrees. Line a sheet pan with parchment paper.

On a floured board, roll the dough to a rectangle a little larger than 10 × 14 inches (see tip). Wrap the dough around your rolling pin and transfer it to the prepared pan. Using a ruler and a small knife, trim the dough to a 10 × 14-inch rectangle. Refrigerate for 15 minutes.

**pro tip** It's important to allow the pastry to "relax" in the fridge for one hour (it's more elastic when you roll it out), but if it's chilled for more time, it will be too hard to roll out. If you overchill dough and then try to bring it back to the right temperature, it will always be too soft on the outside and too hard on the inside. One hour in the fridge is perfect.

**pro tip** Rolling the dough diagonally helps keep the corners square.

*recipe continues*

To peel the peaches, bring a medium pot of water to a boil. Immerse the peaches in the water for between 15 seconds and 3 minutes, depending on ripeness. Transfer them to a bowl of cold water to cool, then remove the skins. Cut the peaches in half, remove the pits, and cut in ½-inch-thick wedges. Remove the stem of each fig and cut them in quarters through the stem (or in sixths, if the figs are very large). Remove the pits from the plums and cut them in ½-inch-thick wedges through the stem. Place the fruit artfully in rows on the dough. Sprinkle with the full ½ cup of sugar and dot with the butter. Bake for 45 minutes to 1 hour, until the pastry is browned and the fruit starts to brown. Rotate the pan once during baking. If the pastry puffs up in one area, cut a little slit with a knife to let the air out. Don't worry! The juices will burn in the pan (see tip) but the tart (and the pan!) will be fine! When the tart's done, loosen it from the pan while it's still warm and transfer it to a board or clean piece of parchment paper.

In a small pan, heat the apricot jelly with 2 tablespoons water and brush the fruit and pastry completely with the mixture. Allow to cool, cut into squares, and serve warm or at room temperature.

# salted caramel sundae

serves 6

*Last year for Christmas I took my team to Jean-Georges Vongerichten's restaurant at Topping Rose House in Bridgehampton, New York. For dessert, we ordered his famous salted caramel sundae. It's sweet and salty peanut caramel popcorn, salted caramel ice cream, and chocolate sauce. It was so crazy delicious that I came right home and made my own version.*

1 cup roasted, salted peanuts

4 cups plain (not butter-flavored) prepared microwave popcorn,
   such as Newman's Own Natural

1½ cups sugar

1 tablespoon light corn syrup

2 teaspoons pure vanilla extract

2 teaspoons kosher salt

1 teaspoon fleur de sel

Chocolate Sauce (recipe follows)

2 pints Talenti Sea Salt Caramel Gelato

Sweetened Whipped Cream (recipe follows)

Preheat the oven to 350 degrees.

Spread the peanuts on a sheet pan and roast for 7 minutes, until they become fragrant. Pour into a medium bowl, add the popcorn, and set aside. Line the sheet pan with parchment paper.

Place the sugar and ¼ cup water in a medium (10-inch) sauté pan and mix with a fork until all the sugar is moistened. Cook over medium-high heat until the sugar dissolves—from this point on, don't stir the caramel, swirl the pan! (Don't worry if the mixture looks as though it's crystallizing.) Continue to cook for 5 to 10 minutes until it becomes a clear golden brown, swirling the pan constantly at the end. (Be careful, the caramel is *very* hot!) Off the heat, quickly add the corn syrup and vanilla (it will bubble up!) and swirl the pan to combine. Working quickly (the caramel will continue to cook in the pan), add the popcorn and nut mixture plus the kosher salt and toss with two large spoons until the popcorn and nuts are completely coated.

Pour the mixture plus any extra caramel in the pan onto the prepared sheet pan and spread the mixture out in one layer, pulling it

**pro tip** When making caramel, if even a grain of sugar drops into the hot mixture, it may cause the caramel to solidify. While you're cooking the mixture, use a wet brush to brush down any stray grains of sugar on the side of the pan.

**make ahead:** Prepare the peanut and popcorn brittle and cool completely. Store in a sealed container at room temperature for up to a week.

*recipe continues*

apart with two forks. Sprinkle with the fleur de sel and set aside to cool. When it's completely cooled, carefully break into large clusters with your hands.

To serve, pour puddles of chocolate sauce into shallow bowls. For each serving, place 3 small scoops of gelato on the chocolate sauce, sprinkle with some of the caramelized popcorn, and add a dollop of the sweetened whipped cream in the middle. Serve immediately.

# chocolate sauce

makes 1½ cups

**8 ounces bittersweet chocolate, roughly chopped**
**1 cup heavy cream**
**2 teaspoons light corn syrup**
**1 teaspoon instant coffee granules, such as Nescafé**

Place the chocolate, cream, corn syrup, and coffee in a bowl set over a pan of simmering water. Be sure the water doesn't touch the bottom of the bowl. Heat the mixture, stirring occasionally, until the chocolate melts and the mixture is smooth. Serve warm.

**pro tip** When chocolate burns, it will seize and turn grainy. Heat it only until it melts, then take the bowl off the double boiler.

**make ahead:** You can keep the sauce warm for up to an hour in a double boiler over simmering water.

# sweetened whipped cream

makes 2 cups

**1 cup cold heavy cream**
**1 tablespoon sugar**
**1 teaspoon pure vanilla extract**

Pour the cream into the bowl of an electric mixer fitted with the whisk attachment. Add the sugar and vanilla and beat on high speed until the cream forms soft peaks.

# fresh berries & sweet ricotta

serves 6

*In the summer, Jeffrey always wants fresh fruit for dessert, but it doesn't seem special enough to serve at a dinner party. Instead, I make homemade ricotta (it's easier than you think!), and mix it with honey and vanilla to serve with fresh berries, along with a drizzle of raspberry sauce. Voilà! Fresh fruit—but so much better!*

**Homemade Ricotta (page 264)**

**2 tablespoons sugar**

**2 tablespoons liquid honey**

**1½ teaspoons pure vanilla extract**

**2 cups fresh strawberries, hulled and halved or sliced, depending on size (see tip)**

**2 (6-ounce) packages fresh raspberries**

**2 (6-ounce) packages fresh blueberries**

**Fresh Raspberry Sauce (page 265)**

**Grated lemon zest, for serving**

Place the ricotta in a medium bowl and stir in the sugar, honey, and vanilla. Set aside at room temperature for up to 2 hours. In another bowl, combine the strawberries, raspberries, and blueberries.

When ready to serve, divide the berries among 6 bowls. With an ice cream scoop, place a large dollop of the ricotta in each bowl and drizzle with lots of the fresh raspberry sauce. Sprinkle with the lemon zest and serve.

**pro tip** When doing a repetitive task such as hulling strawberries, do all the hulling first and then all the slicing. It's faster!

# rum raisin apple strudel
## with rum glaze

serves 8 to 10

*Apple strudel is one of those desserts that sounds really hard to make but after you've done it once, you'll get the hang of it. I love anything rum raisin so I thought this twist on a classic apple strudel might be fabulous. A drizzle of rum glaze at the end makes it even better.*

½ cup golden raisins

⅓ cup dark rum, such as Mount Gay, plus extra for the glaze

½ cup walnuts

½ cup plain dry bread crumbs, such as Progresso

3 large Golden Delicious apples, peeled, cored, and
   ¼ to ½-inch diced (1½ pounds)

6 tablespoons turbinado sugar, such as Sugar in the Raw

3 tablespoons all-purpose flour

2 teaspoons grated lemon zest (2 lemons)

1 tablespoon freshly squeezed lemon juice

¾ teaspoon ground cinnamon

10 tablespoons (1¼ sticks) unsalted butter, melted, divided

¼ teaspoon kosher salt

10 (14 × 18-inch) sheets frozen Kontos phyllo dough, defrosted
   overnight in the refrigerator (see note)

1 cup confectioners' sugar

Preheat the oven to 375 degrees.

Place the raisins and rum in a small bowl, microwave on high for 30 seconds, and set aside. Place the walnuts on a sheet pan and roast for 6 to 8 minutes, tossing once, until lightly browned. Set aside to cool. Transfer to a food processor fitted with the steel blade and process until finely ground. Add the bread crumbs and process *just* until combined. Set aside in a small bowl. Line the sheet pan with parchment paper.

In a medium bowl, combine the apples, turbinado sugar, flour, lemon zest, lemon juice, cinnamon, 2 tablespoons of the melted butter, and the salt. Drain the raisins, reserving the liquid, and add the raisins to the apples.

Kontos phyllo sheets are big enough to make 2 large strudels. If you use Athens phyllo, the sheets are 9 × 13 inches and you will need to make 4 small strudels.

*recipe continues*

Unfold the phyllo dough and cover immediately with a slightly damp kitchen towel. Working quickly, place one sheet of phyllo on a dry work surface with the long edge facing you and re-cover the stack of phyllo with the kitchen towel. Brush the sheet of phyllo lightly with melted butter and sprinkle it evenly with 1 tablespoon of the bread crumb mixture. Place a second sheet of phyllo on top, buttering and sprinkling it with bread crumbs. Repeat until you have 5 layers of phyllo.

Spoon half the apple mixture in a 4-inch-thick log 2 inches inside the long edge facing you and 2 inches inside the side edges. Fold the short sides up and over the log of apples, then fold the long edge next to you up and over the apples, rolling the strudel away from you (pressing lightly!) until the log is enclosed and the seam is on the bottom. Carefully transfer the strudel to the prepared sheet pan. Repeat to make a second roll. Brush both rolls generously with melted butter and make 4 or 5 diagonal slits in each roll for steam to escape. Bake for 25 to 30 minutes, until the strudels are browned and the apple juices are starting to bubble onto the parchment paper. Set aside to cool for 15 minutes.

Whisk together the confectioners' sugar and 2 tablespoons of the reserved rum, adding just enough rum to make a thick, pourable glaze. Drizzle crosswise on the strudel with the whisk or a small spoon and allow to cool completely before cutting each roll diagonally into 4 or 5 pieces, using a serrated knife. Serve warm.

# fresh fig & ricotta cake

serves 8

*This is a classic Italian combination: figs and ricotta. The base is a moist cake made with butter, sour cream, vanilla, and lemon zest. I cut up some fresh figs, arrange them on top, sprinkle them with demerara sugar, and put the cake in the oven. A dollop of crème fraîche served with the warm cake makes it even more special.*

> 10 tablespoons (1¼ sticks) unsalted butter, at room
>     temperature
> 1 cup granulated sugar
> 3 extra-large eggs, at room temperature
> 1 cup fresh whole milk ricotta, at room temperature (see note)
> 2 tablespoons sour cream
> 1 teaspoon pure vanilla extract
> ½ teaspoon grated lemon zest
> 1¼ cups all-purpose flour
> 1 tablespoon baking powder
> 1 teaspoon kosher salt
> 8 large (or 12 medium) fresh figs, stems removed, quartered
>     through the stem
> 1 tablespoon turbinado sugar, such as Sugar in the Raw
> Crème fraîche, for serving

Since ricotta is such an important flavor in this cake, try to use fresh ricotta from an Italian specialty store.

Preheat the oven to 375 degrees. Butter and flour a 9-inch round springform pan, tapping out the excess flour.

Place the butter and granulated sugar in the bowl of an electric mixer fitted with the paddle attachment and beat on medium speed for 3 minutes, until light and fluffy, scraping down the bowl with a rubber spatula. With the mixer on medium low, add the eggs, one at a time, scraping down the bowl and mixing until smooth. Add the ricotta, sour cream, vanilla, and lemon zest and mix until combined. Don't worry; the ricotta will make it look lumpy.

In a small bowl, sift together the flour, baking powder, and salt. With the mixer on low, slowly add the dry ingredients to the batter, mixing just until combined. Pour the batter into the prepared pan and smooth the top. Arrange the figs on the cake, cut sides up, in snug but not

*recipe continues*

overlapping concentric circles. Sprinkle with the turbindo sugar and bake for 35 to 45 minutes, until the top is lightly browned and a toothpick inserted in the center comes out clean.

Allow the cake to cool in the pan on a baking rack for 15 to 20 minutes, transfer to a cake plate, and serve warm with crème fraîche on the side.

# moscato poached fruit

serves 8

*People always ask me about the name Barefoot Contessa. It originally came from a movie starring Ava Gardner and Humphrey Bogart, but for me, it's about being elegant and earthy. I think this recipe is exactly that—all kinds of delicious dried fruit poached in a sweet Italian dessert wine and served with a dollop of crème fraîche. So simple, yet so elegant!*

1 (750-ml) bottle Moscato d'Asti Italian sparkling wine

1½ cups sugar

1 (6-inch) cinnamon stick or 2 (3-inch) sticks

1 vanilla bean, split lengthwise

Zest of 2 large oranges (see tip)

Zest of 1 lemon (see tip)

8 dried cloves, wrapped in cheesecloth and tied with
    kitchen string

2 cups large dried Calmyrna figs, hard stems removed (11 ounces)

2 cups large dried apricots (11 ounces)

1 cup large pitted prunes (6 ounces)

1 cup large dried peaches (6 ounces)

¾ cup dried cherries (5 ounces)

Crème fraîche, for serving

Combine the wine, sugar, cinnamon, vanilla bean, orange zest, and lemon zest in a medium (10 to 11-inch) pot or Dutch oven, such as Le Creuset. Add the bundle of cloves and 2 cups water, bring to a boil, reduce the heat, and simmer uncovered for 15 minutes.

Add the figs, apricots, prunes, and peaches to the simmering liquid and bring to a boil. Lower the heat and simmer uncovered for 15 minutes, stirring occasionally, until all the fruit is tender. (Don't worry if the figs are a little firmer; you don't want to overcook the rest of the fruit.) Discard the bundle of cloves.

Off the heat, stir in the cherries and allow the fruit and liquid to cool to room temperature. Serve warm or at room temperature with the poaching liquid and a dollop of crème fraîche.

**pro tip** A strip zester makes very thin strips of zest so you can see them in the cooked mixture.

**make ahead:** You can prepare the poached fruit, cover, and refrigerate for several days. Reheat and serve warm.

# fresh peach cremolata

serves 6 to 8

*Cremolata is a frozen Italian dessert similar to granita. When peaches are in season, all I do is peel them, puree them, and freeze them with some Grand Marnier and vanilla. You won't believe how fresh and creamy this dish is, without a drop of cream!*

**1½ cups sugar**
**2 pounds fresh ripe peaches (see tip)**
**1 tablespoon Grand Marnier liqueur**
**Seeds scraped from ½ vanilla bean**

Place the sugar and 1½ cups water in a small saucepan and simmer until the sugar dissolves. Set aside.

Fill a large saucepan with water and bring it to a boil. Add the peaches and cook for between 15 seconds and 3 minutes, just until the skins peel off easily. (Ripe peaches will be ready sooner.) Transfer the peaches to a bowl of cool water, peel, and cut in wedges into the bowl of a food processor fitted with the steel blade, discarding the pits. Puree the peaches completely and pour into a 9 × 13-inch baking dish.

Whisk the sugar syrup, Grand Marnier, and vanilla seeds into the peach puree. Place the dish uncovered on a level shelf in the freezer for 30 minutes to one hour, until it begins to crystallize around the edges. Scrape the entire mixture, including the edges, with the tines of a fork and freeze for another 30 minutes. Continue freezing and scraping every 30 minutes, until the mixture is soft-frozen. It should take 2 to 3 hours to freeze and will be good to serve for up to 4 hours afterward. If the mixture gets too frozen, allow it to sit at room temperature for 30 minutes, and scrape it again with a dinner fork. Serve frozen in decorative glasses.

**pro tip** The best way to ripen peaches is to place them in a brown paper bag with the top folded closed, and allow them to sit at room temperature for a day or two.

**make ahead:** Prepare the base and refrigerate for a day or two. Freeze before serving.

# raspberry baked alaska

serves 6

*There are three types of meringues. French meringue is the basic version with egg whites and granulated sugar, Italian meringue uses sugar syrup instead of granulated sugar, and Swiss meringue—which I use here—is made by first heating egg whites and sugar over a double boiler before beating them. It makes a dense, glossy, marshmallow-like meringue, which is perfect over a scoop of ice cream and slice of pound cake to make a baked Alaska. This is a "WOW" dessert that you can make ahead, freeze, and bake just before serving.*

**1 (1-pound) store-bought pound cake**
**1 pint good raspberry sorbet, such as Ciao Bella**
**1 pint good vanilla ice cream, such as Häagen-Dazs**

for the swiss meringue
**8 extra-large egg whites**
**1½ cups sugar**
**2 teaspoons pure vanilla extract**
**½ teaspoon cream of tartar**
**½ teaspoon kosher salt**

**Fresh Raspberry Sauce (page 265)**

Slice the cake into six ½-inch-thick slices. Cut six (2½-inch) circles—one from each slice—with an unfluted round cookie cutter, discarding the scraps. (You can also use a small knife.) Place the cake rounds 2 inches apart on a flat dish that will fit in your freezer.

Soften the sorbet and ice cream just enough to be able to scoop them with a standard 2¼-inch-diameter ice cream scoop (15 to 30 seconds in the microwave works). Fill half the scoop with raspberry sorbet and the rest of the scoop with vanilla ice cream and place an ice cream ball, flat side down, in the middle of each cake round. Freeze for at least 30 minutes, until the ice cream is very hard.

Preheat the oven to 500 degrees.

To make the Swiss meringue, place the egg whites and sugar in a heat-proof glass bowl set over a pan of simmering water. Whisk the mixture almost constantly, until it reaches 120 degrees on a candy thermometer and the sugar has dissolved (see tip). Pour the mixture

 **pro tip** To be sure the sugar has dissolved in the meringue mixture, rub a bit of the egg whites between your fingertips; they shouldn't feel gritty.

*recipe continues*

into the bowl of an electric mixer fitted with the whisk attachment. Add the vanilla, cream of tartar, and salt and beat on medium speed for one minute, then on high speed for 5 minutes, until the egg whites form stiff, glossy peaks.

Transfer the cake rounds and ice cream to a sheet pan lined with parchment paper. Working quickly, spread the meringue with a spoon or small spatula, making lots of peaks all over with the back of the spoon. (You can also use a pastry bag fitted with a large fluted tip and pipe the meringue thickly around each ball of ice cream and cake.) Be sure all of the ice cream is covered with meringue. Bake for 2½ to 3 minutes, until the edges of the meringues are browned, turning the pan once to brown evenly. Transfer to dessert plates, drizzle fresh raspberry sauce around each baked Alaska, and serve immediately.

**make ahead:** You can assemble the baked Alaskas completely and freeze them for a few days—but don't cover them, because the meringue won't freeze hard and you'll ruin the piping. Bake before serving.

# red berry shortcakes
## with honey yogurt

serves 6

*My friend Sarah Chase told me that when she was a kid growing up in Connecticut, one night each year when strawberries were in season her family would have just strawberry shortcakes for dinner! This is a big, crumbly short-cake filled with honey Greek yogurt, lots of berries, and some grated orange zest. Sounds like dinner to me!*

2¼ cups all-purpose flour, plus extra for rolling

¼ cup plus 2 tablespoons granulated sugar, divided

1 tablespoon baking powder

1 teaspoon kosher salt

12 tablespoons (1½ sticks) cold unsalted butter, ½-inch diced

¾ cup cold heavy cream

2 cold extra-large eggs

1½ teaspoons grated orange zest, plus extra for serving

1 egg, beaten with 1 tablespoon water, for egg wash

2 teaspoons turbinado sugar, such as Sugar in the Raw,
   for sprinkling

4 cups strawberries, hulled and thickly sliced (16 ounces)

6 ounces fresh raspberries

2 (7-ounce) containers Greek yogurt, such as Fage

¼ cup liquid honey

6 sprigs fresh mint, for serving

**pro tip** To hull strawberries, use the tip of a paring knife to remove a cone-shaped hull rather than cutting it across the top.

Preheat the oven to 425 degrees. Line a sheet pan with parchment paper.

In the bowl of an electric mixer fitted with the paddle attachment, combine the flour, the 2 tablespoons granulated sugar, the baking powder, and salt. Add the butter and mix at low speed *just* until the butter is the size of peas. In a 2-cup measuring cup, whisk together the heavy cream, eggs, and orange zest. With the mixer on low, add the cream mixture to the flour mixture and mix *just* until combined. The dough will be very sticky.

Heavily flour a cutting board. Mix the dough with a rubber spatula to

*recipe continues*

be sure all of the dry ingredients at the bottom of the bowl are incorporated. Transfer to a board and knead lightly into a disk, adding just enough flour to keep the dough from sticking. Roll or pat the dough ¾ to 1 inch thick. Cut circles of dough with a plain 3-inch round cutter and transfer to the prepared sheet pan. Chill for 30 minutes. Brush the tops with the egg wash and sprinkle with the turbinado sugar. Bake for 18 to 20 minutes, until the tops are browned and spring back when touched. Set aside to cool for 10 minutes.

Meanwhile, combine the strawberries and the ¼ cup granulated sugar in a medium bowl. Set aside at room temperature for 30 minutes. Carefully fold in the raspberries and set aside for another 15 minutes to macerate. In a separate bowl, whisk together the yogurt and honey, cover, and refrigerate.

To assemble, split each shortcake in half horizontally and place the bottoms on dessert plates. Spoon the yogurt mixture on each cake and spoon the berries and their juices on top. Place the shortcake tops over the berries. Sprinkle with extra grated orange zest, garnish with a sprig of mint, and serve.

**pro tip** You can split the shortcakes with a knife, but they're prettier with jagged edges; split them with a fork, as you would an English muffin.

# vanilla roasted rhubarb
## with sweet yogurt

serves 6

*I love to follow Yotam Ottolenghi on Instagram, and one day he posted a dish of roasted rhubarb with a dollop of yogurt and chopped, salted pistachios that looked amazing. I've used rhubarb in pies and crumbles but never roasted it on its own. This recipe is inspired by his: there's something about the vanilla bean and rhubarb roasted together that's just out of this world.*

32 ounces plain whole milk yogurt

5 tablespoons plus ½ cup sugar, divided

Kosher salt

1½ pounds fresh rhubarb

¾ cup Moscato d'Asti Italian sparkling wine

1 vanilla bean, cut in half lengthwise

2 lemons

¼ cup salted, roasted whole shelled pistachios, toasted (see note) and chopped

Place a strainer over a bowl, line it with cheesecloth, spoon in the yogurt, and fold the cheesecloth over to enclose the yogurt. Refrigerate for 3 to 4 hours, discarding the drained liquid from time to time. Transfer the thickened yogurt to a bowl, stir in the 5 tablespoons of sugar and a pinch of salt, and refrigerate.

Preheat the oven to 350 degrees.

Cut the rhubarb in 4-inch batons (cut any thick stalks in half lengthwise so they are all a similar size) and place in a 12 × 10-inch baking dish that holds them snugly. Add the remaining ½ cup of sugar, the Moscato, and the vanilla bean. Peel ¾ of one lemon with a vegetable peeler (don't cut into the bitter white pith), cut the peel into thin julienned strips, and add to the rhubarb. Toss everything together in the baking dish, arrange the rhubarb flat, and roast for 20 to 30 minutes, until the rhubarb is very tender but not mushy.

When ready to serve, place a large dollop of yogurt in the middle of 6 shallow bowls and spoon some rhubarb and the juices around it. Sprinkle with the pistachios and use a Microplane to grate some lemon zest over each serving. Serve at room temperature.

To toast the pistachios, place the nuts on a sheet pan and roast them at 350 degrees for 10 minutes. Set aside to cool.

# daniel rose's pear clafouti

serves 6

*Daniel Rose is an American chef who owns wonderful restaurants in Paris and New York. Daniel made this Pear Clafouti with me; it's amazing how he takes two things as simple as a pear and a pancake batter and, with ingredients you probably have in the pantry, turns them into such an elegant dessert. If you don't have gratin dishes, this can be made in an oval baking dish large enough to hold the pears snuggly.*

**Seeds scraped from 1 vanilla bean**
**2 teaspoons plus ⅔ cup sugar**
**1 tablespoon unsalted butter, at room temperature**
**3 extra-large eggs, at room temperature**
**¼ cup sifted all-purpose flour**
**¾ cup heavy cream**
**¾ cup whole milk**
**1 tablespoon pear brandy**
**Pinch of star anise grated with a Microplane zester**
**¼ teaspoon kosher salt**
**4 ripe Bartlett pears**
**Lime zest, for garnish**

**pro tip** Bartlett pears go from hard to mealy really quickly. Choose pears that are firm and allow them to sit at room temperature until they just yield to firm pressure.

Preheat the oven to 400 degrees. Arrange two racks equally spaced in the oven. Place six (6½-inch) individual gratin dishes on two sheet pans.

In a small bowl, combine the vanilla seeds with the 2 teaspoons of sugar. Spread the butter in the six gratin dishes and sprinkle with the vanilla and sugar mixture. Set aside.

In the bowl of an electric mixer fitted with the paddle attachment, beat the eggs and the remaining ⅔ cup sugar on medium speed, until blended. Lower the speed and add the flour, cream, milk, and brandy. Whisk in the star anise and salt and set aside for 10 minutes. It will be the consistency of pancake batter.

Meanwhile, peel the pears and cut them in half through the stem. Using a melon baller, remove the cores and, using a small paring knife, remove the stems from the center of the pears. With the cut sides down, slice each half crosswise in ¼-inch-thick slices, keeping the pear's shape intact. Transfer half a pear to each gratin dish, fanning them out in overlapping slices down the middle of the dish and using the extra small pieces to fill in the sides. Divide the batter equally among the gratins (the pears will only be half immersed in the batter) and bake for 35 to 40 minutes, until the edges are golden brown and the custard is set. Sprinkle with lime zest and serve hot or warm.

# vanilla brioche bread pudding

serves 9 to 10

*I make this pudding with delicious brioche bread and a rich custard with lots of vanilla extract and vanilla bean. Here's a pro secret for a fast, easy sauce: vanilla ice cream is essentially crème anglaise that's been frozen. I reverse the process and end up with crème anglaise!*

1 (12-ounce) brioche loaf (see note)

3 extra-large whole eggs

8 extra-large egg yolks

4 cups half-and-half

1 cup whole milk

1¼ cups granulated sugar

2 teaspoons pure vanilla extract

Seeds scraped from 1 vanilla bean

Confectioners' sugar, for dusting

2 pints vanilla ice cream, such as Häagen-Dazs, melted

I use Eli's Breads small brioche loaves, which you can order at EliZabar.com.

Preheat the oven to 350 degrees. Space two racks evenly in the oven.

Cut five ¾-inch-thick slices of brioche and place them in one layer on a sheet pan. Trim some of the crusts from the remaining brioche and cut in 1-inch dice. Spread out on a second sheet pan. Put both pans in the oven for 5 minutes, to lightly toast the bread.

Meanwhile, for the custard, whisk together the whole eggs, yolks, half-and-half, milk, granulated sugar, vanilla, and vanilla seeds in a large bowl, and set aside. Line a 10 × 12 × 2-inch rectangular baking dish with the whole slices of brioche, cutting them to fit in one layer. Distribute the diced brioche on top. Pour on the custard and press lightly so all the bread is soaked with custard. Set aside for 10 minutes.

Place the dish in a roasting pan large enough to allow the baking dish to sit flat. Pour about 1 inch of the hottest tap water into the roasting pan, being sure not to get any water into the custard. Cover the roasting pan tightly with aluminum foil, tenting the foil so it doesn't touch the pudding. Cut a few holes in the foil to allow steam to escape. Bake for 45 minutes. Uncover and bake for 45 to 50 minutes, until the custard is set and a knife inserted in the middle comes out clean. Dust with confectioners' sugar and serve warm, drizzled with melted ice cream.

**pro tip** A small sieve is perfect for dusting with confectioners' sugar. Pour the sugar into a sieve over the sink (not the dish!) and tap the edge of the sieve lightly with your hand while holding it over the dish.

# panna cotta with fresh raspberry sauce

serves 7 or 8

*Two of my favorite things to serve together are raspberries and cream. Panna cotta is an old-fashioned Italian pudding (it literally means "cooked milk") that I make with cream, yogurt, and lots of vanilla. I serve it with fresh raspberry sauce and fresh berries. It's my idea of heaven!*

**2 teaspoons (1 packet) unflavored gelatin**

**3 cups heavy cream, divided**

**2 cups plain whole milk yogurt**

**2 teaspoons pure vanilla extract**

**Seeds scraped from 1 vanilla bean**

**¾ cup sugar**

**2 tablespoons Grand Marnier liqueur**

**Fresh Raspberry Sauce (page 265)**

**2 (6-ounce) packages fresh raspberries**

In a small bowl, sprinkle the gelatin on 3 tablespoons cold water. Stir and set aside for 10 minutes to allow the gelatin to dissolve.

Meanwhile, in a large bowl, whisk together 1½ cups of the cream, the yogurt, vanilla extract, and vanilla seeds. Heat the remaining 1½ cups of cream and the sugar in a small saucepan and bring to a simmer over medium heat just until the sugar dissolves. Off the heat, stir the softened gelatin into the hot cream and stir until dissolved. Pour the hot cream and gelatin mixture into the cream and yogurt mixture and stir in the Grand Marnier. Pour into 7 or 8 serving glasses and refrigerate uncovered until cold. When the panna cottas are thoroughly chilled, cover them with plastic wrap and refrigerate overnight.

Before serving, spoon 2 tablespoons of the fresh raspberry sauce on each panna cotta and top with fresh raspberries. Serve cold.

**pro tip** To pour the panna cotta into glasses without drips on the sides, transfer the mixture into a glass measuring cup first and then pour carefully into the center of each glass.

# triple chocolate loaf cakes

makes 2 loaves

*I don't think there's any way I could get more chocolate into this cake. It's got bittersweet chocolate, cocoa powder, and chocolate chips in the batter. This recipe makes two loaves, one for now and one to save for later: you never know when you'll have a chocolate cake emergency! As always, a little coffee brings out the deep chocolate flavor.*

16 tablespoons (2 sticks) unsalted butter, at room temperature

2 cups plus 2 tablespoons all-purpose flour, divided

1 cup boiling water

5 ounces bittersweet chocolate, such as Lindt, roughly chopped

2 tablespoons unsweetened cocoa powder, such as Pernigotti

1 teaspoon instant coffee granules, such as Nescafé

1 teaspoon baking powder

1½ teaspoons kosher salt

1 cup roughly chopped walnuts

1 cup semisweet chocolate chips

1 cup granulated sugar

1 cup dark brown sugar, lightly packed

3 extra-large eggs, at room temperature

2 teaspoons pure vanilla extract

Preheat the oven to 350 degrees. Grease two (8½ × 4½ × 2½-inch) loaf pans, line the bottoms with parchment paper, then grease and flour the pans.

Pour the boiling water into a 2-cup glass measuring cup, add the bittersweet chocolate, cocoa powder, and coffee granules, and stir until the chocolate melts. Set aside to cool for at least 15 minutes.

In a medium bowl, sift together the 2 cups flour, the baking powder, and salt and set aside. In another bowl, combine the walnuts, chocolate chips, and the 2 tablespoons flour and set aside.

In the bowl of an electric mixer fitted with the paddle attachment, beat the butter, granulated sugar, and brown sugar together on medium speed for 2 minutes. With the mixer on low, add the eggs, one at a time, and then the vanilla, scraping down the bowl with a rubber spatula. Alternately in thirds, add the flour mixture and the chocolate mixture, beginning and ending with the flour. Fold in the nut mixture with a rubber spatula. Divide the batter equally between the prepared pans, smooth the tops, and bake for 45 to 55 minutes, until a toothpick inserted in the middle comes out clean. (Test in a few places because you might hit a warm chocolate chip.) Cool in the pans for 30 minutes, turn out on a cooling rack, rounded side up, and allow to cool to room temperature.

# vanilla ice cream with limoncello

serves 6

*I always say, my friends don't have more fun at dinner if I spent all day making the dessert, and this easy recipe proves that rule. I was hosting an Italian dinner party for my friend Antonia Bellanca and I needed a quick dessert. I scooped vanilla ice cream into pretty glass bowls and allowed each person to pour as much limoncello on top as they wanted. Antonia loved it!*

**2 pints good vanilla ice cream, such as Häagen-Dazs**
**Limoncello liqueur, chilled**
**Store-bought biscotti, for serving**

Scoop 2 balls of vanilla ice cream into each of 6 dessert glasses or cups. Pour limoncello over the ice cream and serve with a biscotti on the side.

You can order Eli Zabar's biscotti at EliZabar.com.

breakfast

# prep like a pro

Prepping ingredients before you start to cook may seem like busy work, or an inefficient use of your kitchen time, but believe me, the opposite is true. Having all of your ingredients sliced, diced, or trimmed as needed and ready to add to the pan allows you to cook in a more controlled, thoughtful way. And reviewing the recipe carefully from start to finish before you jump in will save you unnecessary trips back and forth to the fridge (or grocery store!).

Once you've made sure you have all the ingredients you need on hand, prep them as indicated and arrange them on your work surface in small bowls, almost as if you are doing your own cooking demo. Remember, if you're madly trying to dice an onion while your meat is browning in the pot, it's much harder to focus on getting the proper sear. And lining up your seasonings ahead of time means your garlic won't scorch while you're rummaging around the back of your spice cabinet looking for the smoked paprika.

Always take care to cut or chop your ingredients exactly as indicated for the best results. You'll see recipes that call for ingredients to be sliced, large diced, chopped, or minced, and believe it or not, these small nuances make a difference in the final outcome of a dish. Minced onions melt into the sauce, giving it savory body, while sliced onions add texture and a more pronounced onion flavor in each bite. I'm often asked to explain these common cooking terms and I understand why they can be confusing! How much finer is minced parsley than chopped parsley? And exactly what size is "roughly chopped?" The photographs opposite show just what shred, large dice, small dice, and chop mean to me so you can prep your ingredients as I do.

It's also important to use the right tool for the desired result. While you can use a sturdy chef's knife for just about anything from mincing to dicing, the slicing or grating blade of your food processor will save time and effort as well as producing uniformly thin slices of Brussels sprouts or cabbage. And put that paring knife away; you'll work twice as hard to cut a cucumber when you use a smaller blade with less consistent results, trust me!

The next time you make a stew or sauté, try getting your ingredients prepped and ready to go before you fire up the skillet and see if it doesn't make the cooking process go more smoothly and with less stress.

SHRED

LARGE DICE

SMALL DICE

CHOP

# belgian waffles & smoked salmon

makes 10 to 12 large waffles

*I had a breakfast party and made a buffet with waffles, bagels, smoked salmon, and lots of other things. My friend Eli Zabar decided to put crème fraîche and smoked salmon on the waffles instead of the bagels. Everyone started making them! There's something about the warm waffles, salty salmon, and rich crème fraîche that's totally decadent.*

**½ cup warm water (110 to 115 degrees)**

**1 package (¼ ounce) active dry yeast, at room temperature**

**2 teaspoons sugar**

**2 cups lukewarm whole milk (90 to 100 degrees)**

**8 tablespoons (1 stick) unsalted butter, melted, plus extra for the waffle iron**

**2 tablespoons liquid honey**

**1 teaspoon pure vanilla extract**

**1¼ teaspoons kosher salt**

**2 cups all-purpose flour**

**2 extra-large eggs**

**¼ teaspoon baking soda**

**8 ounces thinly sliced smoked salmon, for serving**

**Crème fraîche and minced dill, for serving**

**pro tip** I use a Belgian waffle maker, which makes thicker, more professional-looking waffles. You can also use a standard waffle iron.

**make ahead:** The waffles can be cooked up to one hour ahead and allowed to sit on sheet pans at room temperature. Reheat for 10 minutes in a 350-degree oven, turning once, before serving.

The night before, combine the water, yeast, and sugar in a very large bowl (the batter will expand enormously). Allow it to stand for about 5 minutes, until the yeast dissolves and the mixture has started to foam, which tells you the yeast is alive. Stir in the milk, butter, honey, vanilla, and salt. Add the flour and whisk until the batter is smooth. Cover the bowl with plastic wrap and allow it to sit overnight at a cool room temperature.

The next day, preheat the oven to 200 degrees. Heat a Belgian waffle iron according to the manufacturer's instructions and brush the top and bottom with melted butter. Beat the eggs together with the baking soda and whisk them into the batter until combined. Pour just enough of the batter onto the hot waffle iron to cover the grids (⅓ to

½ cup each, depending on your waffle maker), close, and cook for 5 to 6 minutes on medium heat, until the waffles are golden brown. Cut them apart with a small knife, if necessary, and remove them with a fork. Keep warm in the oven while you make more waffles, repeating the process until all the batter has been used. Serve the waffles hot with the smoked salmon and crème fraîche.

# fresh blueberry rhubarb jam

makes 4 cups

*When rhubarb and blueberries are in season, it's so easy to make a big pot of this jam while you're puttering around the house. There are so many ways I love to serve it—on toast, swirled into yogurt, and even on a cheese platter. I might also have been known to sneak a spoonful right from the pot.*

**2½ cups sugar**

**3 tablespoons cassis liqueur, such as Mathilde**

**5 cups (1-inch-diced) fresh rhubarb (about 1½ pounds)**

**1½ cups fresh blueberries (see tip)**

**½ Granny Smith apple, peeled, cored, and small-diced**

**1 tablespoon grated lemon zest (2 lemons)**

Place the sugar and cassis in a large (8 × 4-inch) heavy-bottomed saucepan. Add the rhubarb, blueberries, apple, and lemon zest and toss well to coat the fruit with the cassis and sugar. Cover the pot and cook over medium heat for 5 to 10 minutes, until there is a lot of liquid and it comes to a full boil. Lower the heat and cook uncovered at a low boil for 35 to 40 minutes, stirring occasionally, until the fruit has disintegrated and the mixture has thickened. (I test a little by putting some jam in a dish in the freezer to check the consistency when it cools.) If necessary, cook for another 5 minutes. Set aside to cool, then refrigerate.

**pro tip** Make this only when blueberries are in season. Out-of-season blueberries can have a metallic taste that will ruin the flavor of the jam.

**make ahead:** This jam will last for several weeks in the fridge.

# lemon ricotta pancakes with figs

makes 14 pancakes

*Pancakes can be pretty bland; usually it's about what you put on them rather than what you put in them. These pancakes are so flavorful with ricotta, lemon zest, and vanilla plus the fresh figs on top. If figs are out of season, you can also make these with fresh blueberries.*

1 cup fresh whole milk ricotta

1 cup buttermilk, shaken

3 extra-large eggs

¼ cup sugar

1½ tablespoons grated lemon zest (2 lemons), plus extra
    for serving

¼ cup freshly squeezed lemon juice

½ teaspoon pure vanilla extract

1¼ cups all-purpose flour

¼ cup cornstarch

1 tablespoon baking powder

1½ teaspoons kosher salt

6 tablespoons clarified butter (see tip)

8 to 10 ripe figs, ½-inch diced

Salted butter and pure maple syrup, for serving

In a large bowl, whisk together the ricotta, buttermilk, eggs, sugar, lemon zest, lemon juice, and vanilla. In a medium bowl, whisk together the flour, cornstarch, baking powder, and salt. While stirring with a rubber spatula, add the flour mixture to the ricotta mixture and mix *just* until combined. Set aside for 5 minutes.

Heat a large (12-inch) sauté pan over medium heat. Pour in a table-spoon or two of the clarified butter and heat until the butter sizzles. Stir the batter with a rubber spatula. Using a standard (2¼-inch) ice cream scoop, drop level scoopfuls of batter into the pan and allow them to cook for a few minutes, until bubbles appear all over the top. While the pancakes cook, distribute the figs on the pancakes, then turn to cook on the other side, until they spring back when lightly touched. Repeat with the remaining batter, adding clarified butter to the pan as needed. Transfer to plates, sprinkle with lemon zest, dot with butter, and drizzle with maple syrup. Serve hot.

**pro tip**   Clarified butter has a higher burning temperature than regular butter so pancakes get nicely browned without burning. To clarify butter, melt unsalted butter in a measuring cup in a microwave. Allow the milk solids to settle to the bottom and use just the golden liquid on top. Discard the milk solids.

# shakshuka with feta

serves 4 to 6

*Shakshuka is a dish of eggs poached on a spicy tomato sauce with peppers and onions. It originated in North Africa and became really popular in the Middle East. It seems to be popping up on menus everywhere in the United States.*

**pro tip** Holding the pepper upright, cut down the sides and dice. You'll have flat diced peppers that look more professional.

3 tablespoons good olive oil

1½ cups chopped yellow onion (1 large)

2 cups chopped fennel bulb, top and core removed (1 medium)

1 Holland orange bell pepper, seeded and ½-inch diced

1 poblano pepper, seeded and ½-inch diced (about ½ cup)

1 jalapeño pepper, seeded and minced (about ¼ cup)

1 tablespoon minced garlic (3 cloves)

1 teaspoon smoked Spanish paprika

1 (28-ounce) can diced tomatoes and juices, such as San Marzano

½ cup strained or pureed tomatoes, such as Pomì

Kosher salt and freshly ground black pepper

6 extra-large eggs

5 ounces feta, crumbled

2 tablespoons roughly chopped fresh parsley

Whole-wheat pita bread, toasted, for serving

Preheat the oven to 375 degrees.

Heat the oil in a large (12-inch) ovenproof sauté pan over medium heat. Add the onion, fennel, bell pepper, poblano pepper, and jalapeño pepper and cook over medium to medium-high heat for 10 to 12 minutes, stirring occasionally, until the vegetables are tender and starting to brown. Stir in the garlic and paprika and cook for one minute.

Add the diced tomatoes, strained tomatoes, 2 teaspoons salt, and 1 teaspoon black pepper. Bring to a boil, lower the heat, and simmer for 15 minutes, until the sauce thickens, stirring occasionally.

Off the heat, carefully break the eggs, one at a time, into a small bowl and slide them onto the vegetable mixture. Crumble the feta around the eggs, sprinkle with salt and pepper, and bake for 15 to 20 minutes, until the egg whites are firm but the yolks are still runny. Sprinkle with the parsley and serve from the pan with the pita bread.

# italian iced coffee

makes 2 or 3 drinks

*Jeffrey and I went to Florence with our friends the Libermans and stayed at the beautiful Lungarno Hotel right on the Arno River. When we went down for break-fast one morning, Jeffrey asked the waitress for iced coffee, and she brought him the most delicious iced coffee he'd ever had. In fact, it looked so good that everyone in the restaurant started ordering it. When we got home, I made my own version with espresso, milk, sugar, and a dusting of cocoa powder.*

**⅔ cup hot espresso or strong brewed coffee, regular or decaf**
**2 tablespoons turbinado sugar, such as Sugar in the Raw**
**⅓ cup whole milk or half-and-half**
**1½ cups ice cubes**
**Unsweetened cocoa powder, such as Pernigotti**

Place the hot coffee and the sugar in a measuring cup and stir until the sugar dissolves. Add the milk and pour the mixture into a blender. Add the ice and blend on high speed for 45 to 60 seconds, until the ice cubes have completely dissolved and the mixture is smooth and creamy. Pour into 2 or 3 small glasses, dust lightly with the cocoa powder, and drink ice cold.

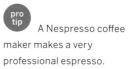 A Nespresso coffee maker makes a very professional espresso.

# morning glory muffins

makes 14 to 16 muffins

*We used to make so many of these muffins at Barefoot Contessa! They're filled with carrots, apple, pineapple, pecans, and coconut—kind of like eating carrot cake, without the frosting. Our recipe was inspired by muffins that were originally made at the Morning Glory Café on Nantucket.*

1 cup vegetable oil, plus extra for the pan (see tip)
3 extra-large eggs
2 teaspoons pure vanilla extract
2 cups grated carrots, unpeeled and grated on a box grater
1 Granny Smith apple, unpeeled and grated on a box grater
1 (8-ounce) can crushed pineapple, drained
½ cup pecans, roughly chopped
½ cup sweetened shredded coconut
½ cup raisins
2¼ cups all-purpose flour
1¼ cups sugar
1 tablespoon ground cinnamon
2 teaspoons baking soda
1 teaspoon kosher salt

**pro tip** Brush the tops of the muffin pans with oil and the muffins will be easier to remove.

**make ahead:** You can make the batter a day ahead, refrigerate it, then scoop and bake the muffins in the morning.

Preheat the oven to 350 degrees and arrange two racks evenly spaced in the oven. Line two muffin pans with paper muffin cups.

In a large bowl, whisk together the eggs, oil, and vanilla. Add the carrots, apple, pineapple, pecans, coconut, and raisins and stir together. In a medium bowl, sift together the flour, sugar, cinnamon, baking soda, and salt. Add the dry ingredients to the wet ingredients and stir just until combined. Scoop the batter with a standard (2¼-inch) ice cream scoop (I use rounded scoops of batter) into the prepared muffin cups. Bake for 30 to 35 minutes, until a toothpick comes out clean. Place the pans on a baking rack to cool and serve the muffins warm or at room temperature.

# short rib hash & eggs

serves 4

*This is a very flexible recipe made with potatoes, bacon, and onions. I've used leftover short ribs (page 119), but you can substitute brisket, roast beef, pulled pork, kielbasa, or ham plus vegetables like broccoli and kale. It's a great way to clean out the fridge and have an amazing breakfast at the same time!*

1 pound Yukon Gold potatoes, unpeeled, ¾-inch diced

2 teaspoons good white wine vinegar

Kosher salt and freshly ground black pepper

4 ounces thick-cut applewood-smoked bacon, ½-inch diced

Good olive oil

2 cups sliced yellow onion (2 onions)

2 cups (1-inch-diced) cooked boneless short ribs

6 ounces Brussels sprouts, halved, cored, and thinly sliced (see tip)

½ teaspoon Sriracha

1 tablespoon unsalted butter

4 extra-large eggs

4 (½-inch-thick) slices bread from a country loaf, toasted

2 tablespoons minced fresh chives, for serving

**pro tip** Instead of slicing the Brussels sprouts by hand, place them in the feed tube of a food processor fitted with the slicing disk and process.

Place the potatoes in a medium saucepan and add water to cover by 2 inches, plus the vinegar and 2 teaspoons salt. Bring to a boil, lower the heat, and simmer for 5 minutes. Drain and set aside.

Meanwhile, heat a large (12-inch) sauté pan over medium heat, add the bacon, and sauté for 6 to 8 minutes, until lightly browned. Transfer the bacon to a plate using a slotted spoon. Put the potatoes in the sauté pan and cook over medium to medium-high heat, tossing occasionally with a spatula, for 6 to 8 minutes, until the potatoes are lightly browned. If the pan is dry, add a few tablespoons olive oil. Return the bacon to the pan and add the onions, 2 teaspoons salt, and 1 teaspoon pepper, toss well, and cook over medium heat for 8 minutes, tossing occasionally. Add the short ribs, Brussels sprouts, and Sriracha, and cook for 3 to 4 minutes, tossing occasionally, until heated through and the sprouts are crisp-tender.

Meanwhile, melt the butter in a medium (10-inch) sauté pan. Carefully crack 4 eggs into the opposite corners of the pan, sprinkle with salt and pepper, and cook over medium heat for 3 to 4 minutes, until the whites are almost cooked. Cover the pan and cook over low heat for one minute, until the whites are set but the yolks are still runny.

Spoon the hash onto 4 dinner plates, place each egg on a piece of toast, and place one on each plate. Sprinkle with chives and salt and serve hot.

# smoked salmon tartines

serves 4

*Barbara, Lidey, and I love going on book tour because we get to travel to great places. One morning, we had breakfast at the Four Seasons Resort in Scottsdale, Arizona, and I ordered their smoked salmon toast. I loved the whole-grain bread with sliced avocado, smoked salmon, and a slightly sweet mustard and dill sauce.*

**8 slices whole-grain bread, sliced ¼ inch thick, toasted (see note)**
**2 ripe avocados, seeded, peeled, and sliced crosswise**
    **¼ inch thick**
**1 lemon, halved**
**Kosher salt and freshly ground black pepper**
**8 slices smoked salmon (about 8 ounces)**
**Gravlax Sauce (recipe follows)**
**1 small red onion, halved and thinly sliced crosswise in**
    **half-rounds**
**Dill fronds, for serving**

Place the toasted bread on a cutting board and overlap slices of avocado on each piece of bread, using a quarter to half an avocado for each, depending on the sizes of the avocado and the bread. Sprinkle the avocado with lemon juice, then sprinkle with salt and pepper. Place one large slice of salmon on top, ribboning it to fit. Drizzle with a tablespoon of the sauce. Garnish with some red onion, sprinkle with the dill fronds, salt, and pepper, and serve with extra sauce on the side.

I use Eli's Bread's delicious
2-pound health loaf.
You can order it from
EliZabar.com.

# gravlax sauce

makes ¾ cup

2 tablespoons Dijon mustard

1 tablespoon honey mustard

1 teaspoon whole-grain mustard

½ teaspoon ground mustard

1½ tablespoons sugar

2½ tablespoons good white wine
vinegar

2½ tablespoons good olive oil

1½ tablespoons grapeseed oil

2 tablespoons minced fresh dill

½ teaspoon kosher salt

**make ahead:** The sauce may be prepared ahead and refrigerated for up to a week.

Whisk together the Dijon mustard, honey mustard, whole-grain mustard, ground mustard, sugar, and vinegar in a medium bowl. Combine the olive and grapeseed oils in a small measuring cup. Slowly add the oil mixture to the mustard mixture, whisking constantly, until emulsified. Stir in the dill and salt.

# truffled scrambled eggs

serves 3

*I had always made scrambled eggs over medium-high heat, but once I learned to cook them the French way—over very low heat—I was hooked. The eggs come out soft and fluffy, like big scrambled egg clouds. I make this on New Year's Day for an easy but "fancy" brunch.*

1½ tablespoons unsalted butter, at room temperature

8 extra-large eggs

¼ cup half-and-half or whole milk

Kosher salt and freshly ground black pepper

1 tablespoon Urbani white truffle butter, at room temperature (see note)

3 slices brioche bread, toasted

Minced fresh chives, for serving

Order truffle butter online from Urbani.com and store it in the freezer.

Place a medium (10-inch) sauté pan over low heat. Add the butter and allow it to melt but not completely. In a large bowl, whisk together the eggs, half-and-half, 1 teaspoon salt, and ¼ teaspoon pepper until the yolks and whites are just blended. Pour the mixture into the pan but don't mix it.

Allow the eggs to warm slowly over low to medium-low heat without stirring them. This may take 3 to 5 minutes, so be patient! As soon as the eggs start to cook on the bottom, turn the heat to low and, using a rubber spatula to scrape the bottom of the pan, fold the cooked eggs over the uncooked eggs. Once the eggs start to look a little custardy, stir them rapidly with the spatula until they have the texture of very big custardy clouds. Remove the pan from the heat before the eggs are fully cooked and immediately stir the truffle butter into the eggs.

Cut the toast in half diagonally and place the slices on 3 dinner plates. Spoon the scrambled eggs over the toasts, sprinkle with the minced chives and a little salt, and serve hot.

# chocolate pecan scones

makes 14 to 16 large scones

*Okay, I have a thing about scones. When they're good, they're light and flaky and full of flavor. Be sure to use really good chocolate that you dice by hand so there are puddles of melted chocolate when you bite into them. And trust me, four teaspoons of Diamond Crystal kosher salt may sound like a lot but it makes all the difference.*

**3 tablespoons plus 4 cups all-purpose flour, divided**

**1½ cups medium-diced bittersweet chocolate, such as Lindt (8 ounces)**

**1 cup chopped pecans**

**2 tablespoons sugar, plus additional for sprinkling**

**2 tablespoons baking powder**

**4 teaspoons kosher salt**

**¾ pound cold unsalted butter, ½-inch diced**

**1 cup cold heavy cream**

**4 extra-large eggs, lightly beaten**

**1 egg beaten with 2 tablespoons water or cream, for egg wash**

**pro tip** Cold bits of butter in the dough ensure flaky scones. When the heat hits the bits of butter, the water in the butter turns to steam and makes the dough rise.

Preheat the oven to 400 degrees. Arrange two racks evenly spaced in the oven. Line two sheet pans with parchment paper.

In a small bowl, combine the 3 tablespoons flour with the chocolate and pecans and set aside.

In the bowl of an electric mixer fitted with the paddle attachment, combine the 4 cups flour, the sugar, baking powder, and salt. Add the butter and, with the mixer on low speed, blend until the butter is the size of peas. Measure the cream in a 2-cup glass measuring cup, add the eggs, and beat until combined. With the mixer still on low, pour the wet mixture into the dry mixture and combine *just* until blended. Add the chocolate and pecan mixture and mix *just* until combined. The dough will be very sticky.

Dump the dough out onto a very well-floured surface and knead it a few times to be sure the chocolate and pecans are well distributed, adding a little flour so the dough doesn't stick to the board. Flour your hands and a rolling pin and roll the dough ¾ to 1 inch thick. You should see lumps of butter in the dough. Cut the dough with a 3-inch plain round cutter and place the scones on the prepared sheet pans. Reroll the scraps and cut out more scones. Brush the tops with the egg wash, sprinkle with sugar, and bake for 20 minutes, switching the pans halfway through, until the tops are lightly browned and the insides are fully baked. Serve warm or at room temperature.

**make ahead:** You can prepare the dough, cut out the scones, refrigerate them, covered, and bake them the following day.

pro basics

# vegetable stock

makes 4 quarts

*From time to time, we all have a guest who's vegetarian. I'm always looking for a vegetable stock that has the same deep rich flavors as chicken stock to use in so many of my soups. Lidey and I spent a lot of time working on this and I think we've come up with a perfect solution.*

¼ cup good olive oil

8 shallots, halved lengthwise and sliced ¼ inch thick

2 leeks, white and green parts, halved lengthwise and sliced
    ¼ inch thick

2 cups dry white wine, such as Pinot Grigio

8 carrots, unpeeled and chopped

6 large celery stalks with leaves, chopped

4 parsnips, unpeeled and chopped

1 pound cremini mushrooms, halved or quartered

1 small fennel bulb, chopped

20 sprigs fresh parsley

15 sprigs fresh thyme

2 bay leaves

1 head garlic, unpeeled and cut in half crosswise

Kosher salt and freshly ground black pepper

2 teaspoons whole black peppercorns (not ground)

Heat the olive oil in a 16 to 20-quart stockpot. Add the shallots and leeks and cook over medium heat for 8 to 10 minutes, stirring occasionally, until the vegetables start to brown. Add the wine and cook for 2 minutes, scraping up the brown bits in the pan and reducing the wine by half.

Add the carrots, celery, parsnips, mushrooms, and fennel and cook for 8 to 10 minutes, stirring occasionally, until the vegetables start to soften. Add 6 quarts water, the parsley, thyme, bay leaves, garlic, 2 tablespoons salt, and the whole black peppercorns. Bring to a boil, lower the heat, and simmer for 1½ hours. Add 1 tablespoon salt and 1 teaspoon ground black pepper and taste for seasonings. Set aside until cool enough to handle.

Strain the contents of the pot through a colander or sieve and discard the solids. Cool completely and refrigerate the stock for up to a week or freeze for up to 6 months.

# chicken stock

makes 6 quarts

*I have to include this recipe in every book because it's the basis for so many of my dishes. Of course you can use store-bought stock or broth; but this is easy to make and the difference it makes in the finished dish is astonishing. When I'm at home, I throw everything into a big pot and let it simmer away. Four hours later, I have quarts of chicken stock to store in the freezer and the house smells wonderful.*

**3 (5-pound) roasting chickens**

**3 large yellow onions, unpeeled and quartered**

**6 carrots, unpeeled and halved crosswise**

**4 celery stalks with leaves, cut into thirds crosswise**

**4 parsnips, unpeeled and halved crosswise**

**20 sprigs fresh parsley**

**15 sprigs fresh thyme**

**20 sprigs fresh dill**

**1 head garlic, unpeeled and cut in half crosswise**

**2 tablespoons kosher salt**

**2 teaspoons whole black peppercorns (not ground)**

Place the chickens, onions, carrots, celery, parsnips, parsley, thyme, dill, garlic, salt, and peppercorns in a 16 to 20-quart stockpot. Add 7 quarts water and bring to a boil. Lower the heat and simmer uncovered for 4 hours, skimming off any foam that comes to the top. Set aside until cool enough to handle. Strain the entire contents of the pot through a sieve or colander and discard the solids.

Cool completely, skim off the fat, pack in quart containers, and refrigerate for up to a week or freeze for up to 6 months.

# beef stock

makes 5 quarts

*I think canned beef stock never has the deep, rich flavor of roasted beef bones simmered with vegetables, garlic, and red wine. Trust me, when you start making your own stocks, your cooking will be so much better!*

Ask your butcher for marrow and neck bones cut in 2-inch pieces.

**3 pounds marrow bones, cut in 2-inch pieces**
**2 pounds neck bones, cut in 2-inch pieces**
**2 pounds short ribs on the bone, cut in 2-inch pieces**
**6 carrots, unpeeled and ¾-inch diced**
**4 large celery stalks, chopped**
**3 yellow onions, chopped**
**1 head garlic, unpeeled and cut in half horizontally**
**2 cups dry red wine**
**6 ounces tomato paste**
**3 bay leaves**
**20 sprigs fresh parsley**
**15 sprigs fresh thyme**
**1 tablespoon whole black peppercorns (not ground)**
**Kosher salt and freshly ground black pepper**

Preheat the oven to 425 degrees. Place the marrow bones, neck bones, and short ribs in a large roasting pan and roast, turning occasionally, for 45 minutes, until browned. Transfer the bones to a very large (16 to 20-quart) stockpot, leaving the fat in the pan. Add the carrots, celery, onions, and garlic to the roasting pan, toss with the fat, and roast for 15 to 20 minutes, until softened. Add the vegetables to the stockpot.

Add the wine to the roasting pan and cook over medium heat to deglaze the pan, stirring to scrape up the brown bits. Add the mixture to the stockpot along with the tomato paste, bay leaves, parsley, thyme, whole black peppercorns, and 4 tablespoons salt. Add 6 quarts water, bring to a boil, lower the heat, and simmer for 2 hours, skimming the fat occasionally. Stir in 1 teaspoon ground pepper and taste for seasonings. Set aside until cool enough to handle. Strain the contents of the pot through a colander or sieve and discard the solids.

Cool completely, skim off the fat, pack in quart containers, and refrigerate for up to a week or freeze for up to 6 months.

# seafood stock

makes 1 quart

*Many recipes that call for seafood stock say that you can substitute bottled clam juice, but it's not really the same thing. Good seafood stock is full of the flavors of vegetables, fresh herbs, and white wine. It's so worth the effort!*

**2 tablespoons good olive oil**

**Shells from 1 pound large shrimp (see tip)**

**2 cups chopped yellow onion (2 onions)**

**2 carrots, unpeeled and chopped**

**3 celery stalks, chopped**

**2 garlic cloves, minced**

**½ cup dry white wine, such as Pinot Grigio**

**⅓ cup tomato paste**

**10 sprigs fresh thyme**

**Kosher salt and freshly ground black pepper**

Warm the oil in a medium pot set over medium heat. Add the shrimp shells, onions, carrots, and celery and cook for 15 minutes, until lightly browned. Add the garlic and cook for one more minute. Add 1½ quarts water, the wine, tomato paste, thyme, 1 tablespoon salt, and 1½ teaspoons pepper. Bring to a boil, lower the heat, and simmer for one hour. Strain through a sieve, pressing on the solids. You should have approximately 1 quart of stock. If not, add enough water or white wine to make 1 quart.

Cool completely, transfer to containers, and refrigerate for up to 3 days or freeze for up to 1 month.

**pro tip** After peeling shrimp, save the shells in the freezer in an airtight container for making seafood stock.

# perfect poached lobster

makes 1 pound cooked lobster meat

*It's always easier to buy cooked lobster meat rather than dealing with large pots of boiling water and all those pesky shells, but cooked lobster meat from the store can sometimes be a little tough. Mark Bittman suggests cooking lobsters yourself, using an instant-read thermometer to test when they're done. The lobster turns out tender and delicious every time.*

**Kosher salt**
**2 (2-pound) lobsters (see tip)**

Fill a very large (18 to 20-quart) stockpot ¾ full with water, add 2 tablespoons of salt, cover, and bring to a full rolling boil. Immerse the lobsters in the water and cook for 10 minutes, until an instant-read thermometer inserted into the middle of the underside of a tail registers 140 degrees. (Don't worry if the water doesn't come back to a boil.) Remove the lobsters with tongs and set aside until cool enough to handle. Remove the lobster meat from the shell, including the claws.

**pro tip** I ask the seafood shop to kill the lobsters for me, but they must be cooked very soon afterward. To do it at home, place the tip of a large chef's knife exactly where the head and tail connect and plunge it quickly into the lobster. You'll sever the spinal cord and the lobsters won't suffer.

# homemade ricotta

makes about 2 cups

*Of course you can buy ricotta at a grocery store, but homemade ricotta is so delicious and so easy that it's worth making. You can drain it for less time, which makes it moist and creamy, or drain it a little longer if you prefer a firm ricotta. Both are absolutely delicious!*

**4 cups whole milk**
**2 cups heavy cream**
**1 teaspoon kosher salt**
**3 tablespoons good white wine vinegar**

Set a fine-mesh sieve over a deep bowl. Dampen 2 pieces of cheesecloth with water and line the sieve with a double layer of the cheesecloth.

Pour the milk and cream into a medium stainless-steel or enameled pot, such as Le Creuset, and stir in the salt. Bring to a *full rolling* boil over medium heat, stirring occasionally. Turn off the heat and pour in the vinegar. Allow the mixture to stand for one minute, until it curdles. It will separate into thick parts (the curds) and milky parts (the whey).

Pour the mixture into the cheesecloth-lined sieve and allow it to drain into the bowl at room temperature for 20 minutes (for soft ricotta) to 25 minutes (for firmer ricotta), occasionally discarding the liquid that collects in the bowl. Transfer the ricotta to a bowl, discarding the cheesecloth and any remaining liquid. Use immediately or cover with plastic wrap and refrigerate. The ricotta will keep, refrigerated, for 4 to 5 days.

# fresh raspberry sauce

makes 2 cups

*Raspberry sauce is a staple of my dessert repertoire and it's so easy to make. If you have raspberries that you think might go bad, just turn them into this delicious sauce and they'll last for at least another week in the fridge. I use this as a quick dessert poured over ice cream and as a drizzle on fresh fruit, as in my Panna Cotta with Fresh Raspberry Sauce (page 222), Fresh Berries & Sweet Ricotta (page 195), and Raspberry Baked Alaska (page 209).*

**1 (6-ounce) package fresh raspberries**

**½ cup sugar**

**1 cup (12 ounces) seedless raspberry jam, such as Tiptree (see note)**

**1 tablespoon framboise liqueur**

Place the raspberries, sugar, and ¼ cup water in a small saucepan over medium heat. Bring to a boil, lower the heat, and simmer for 4 minutes. Pour the cooked raspberries, the jam, and the framboise into the bowl of a food processor fitted with the steel blade and process until smooth. Pour into a container and chill. The sauce can be refrigerated for up to one week.

If you can't find seedless raspberry jam, you can heat 12 ounces of raspberry jam with seeds over medium heat and strain it through a sieve. Be sure to use real jam, not a "fruit spread."

# homemade vanilla extract

makes about 1 quart

*It was my friend Anna Pump who first taught me to make my own vanilla extract and now I've had my home "brew" going for more than thirty-five years! I just love knowing I have a big stash of vanilla extract and softened vanilla beans sitting on a shelf in the pantry.*

**12 to 24 whole vanilla beans**
**4 cups vodka, such as Smirnoff**

Find a jar with a very tightly sealed lid that will hold at least a dozen vanilla beans straight and upright. I use a 1-liter canning (Ball) jar with a rubber gasket. Place the beans in the jar and pour in enough vodka to cover the beans. Allow the beans to marinate in the vodka at room temperature for at least a few months. You will have two wonderful ingredients for cooking and baking: first, the vodka will become vanilla extract, and almost more importantly, you can snip off one end of a vanilla bean and squeeze out all of the seeds when you are making something that you want to have extra vanilla flavor, such as vanilla cakes, ice cream, or sauces. You can continue this brew for years by adding more vanilla beans and more vodka as you use them.

# time like a pro

In my recipes the recommended internal temperatures indicate when meat should be removed from the oven and left to rest under foil, *not* when it is fully cooked. As it rests, residual heat will continue to cook the meat and bring it to the target temps listed below. It's important to note that guidelines for cooking meat have changed in recent years. At one time people were afraid that rare or undercooked meat might carry diseases, particularly pork, which was associated with trichinosis. To ensure safety it had to be cooked to 180 degrees, which resulted in overcooked, dry meat. Now that trichinosis is no longer a danger, I cook pork to 137 or 140 degrees and it comes out rosy, moist, and delicious.

| | |
|---|---|
| Beef | 125 to 130 degrees for medium rare |
| Chicken | 140 to 145 degrees for chicken breasts / 155 to 160 degrees for thighs or whole chickens |
| Pork | 137 to 140 degrees for medium rare |
| Lamb | 125 for medium rare |
| Duck | 120 degrees for rare |

# swap like a pro

I can't tell you how many times someone has told me they tried one of my recipes "with a few small changes" and wasn't happy with the outcome. Swapping ingredients doesn't always work—if a sauce calls for one cup of heavy cream and you decide to use skim milk instead, it will curdle and never thicken. (Not to mention that it just won't taste the same!) If you want to change a recipe, I recommend following the recipe as written first to understand how it works, then make adjustments the next time. That said, if you're about to start cooking and realize you're missing a key ingredient, the substitutions below will save you a run to the grocery store without compromising on flavor.

| for | substitute |
|---|---|
| Diamond Crystal kosher salt (the only kind I use) | Roughly 50% as much Morton's kosher salt or fine table or sea salt; you'll need to taste, but all of these alternatives are significantly denser and therefore "saltier" than Diamond Crystal |
| White wine | Dry vermouth |
| Shallot, 1 large | ½ small onion and ½ garlic clove |
| Fresh spinach | Baby arugula |
| Chipotle in adobo | Tomato paste plus a pinch each of smoked paprika and cayenne |
| Sriracha | Ketchup with a squeeze of lime and a pinch of cayenne |
| Capers | Green olives |
| Baking powder | ¼ cup cream of tartar plus 2 tablespoons baking soda |
| Cake flour | 1 cup minus 2 tablespoons all-purpose flour plus 2 tablespoons cornstarch |
| Buttermilk | Whole milk (or plain yogurt) with a squeeze of lemon juice |
| Sour cream | Greek yogurt, or cream cheese beaten with a little milk |
| Honey | Maple syrup |
| Brown sugar | White sugar plus molasses (more for dark brown, less for light brown) |

# index

# recipe index